SEEDENOMICS

The Financial Foundation For The Kingdom Of God!

Dr. James Payne

WESTBOW
PRESS®
A DIVISION OF THOMAS NELSON
& ZONDERVAN

WestBow Press books may be ordered through booksellers or by contacting:

WestBow Press
A Division of Thomas Nelson & Zondervan
1663 Liberty Drive
Bloomington, IN 47403
www.westbowpress.com
844-714-3454

ISBN: 978-1-6642-7259-0 (sc)
ISBN: 978-1-6642-7260-6 (hc)
ISBN: 978-1-6642-7258-3 (e)

Library of Congress Control Number: 2022913251

Print information available on the last page.

WestBow Press rev. date: 08/12/2022

Foreword

Get ready for explosive information on one of the most neglected and evaded truths in God's Word! Dr. James Payne's book on Seedenomics will take you beyond the realm of experimenting with the teaching of seedtime and harvest! The revelation in this book will launch you into the manifestation of prosperity in the proportion God has always wanted you to experience!

For years, we have merely attempted to operate in this concept, but now—through Seedenomics—Dr. James Payne carries us beyond what former teachers and preachers have expounded! He clearly and simply explains what farmers and horticulturists know about the mysterious methods of super multiplication. Having written fifty-two books, pamphlets, and workbooks on Biblical Economics over the past twenty-five years, it is my opinion that Dr. Payne's book takes us beyond anything revealed to us on this subject previously.

Prior to now, we have only scratched the surface of the subject of seedtime and harvest. Dr. Payne methodically and masterfully compares the natural with the spiritual by using the forty-three parables of Jesus, pointing out that they were taught to primarily farmers. He tells us that approximately 97% of the economy in Jesus' day was agricultural! With the information in this book at your fingertips, you can now move into the "more than you can ask or think" dimension of Christianity.

Make no mistake about it, for as long as the Lord tarries His coming, this book, *Seedenomics,* will hold a place in the libraries of those who believe God wants to prosper His children. It will be a textbook for speakers, teachers, and preachers, as well as a guideline for Christian businessmen and their employees. Having heard Dr.

Payne speak on this subject many times, it is my honor to write the foreword for *Seedenomics*! James has been like a son to me, and I want to thank him for taking the revelation God gave me well beyond the level God allowed me to take it.

Dr. John Avanzini
Corpus Christie, Texas

Introduction

My mother and father had nine children. I was number eight. My parents and my siblings are all wonderful people. My dad was a factory worker, and my mom did washing and ironing for other people to help supplement the income. They never owned a house, so we moved a lot when I was a kid. They were both hard-working people, but they could never get ahead and make ends meet.

In elementary school, I learned the reproach that comes from poverty. The school bought shoes and clothes for me and occasionally gave me my lunch because my parents could not afford to do so. We were looked down on by neighbors because we always lived in the worst house in the neighborhood.

I started drinking alcohol when I was eleven years old just to try to deal with the pain I felt inside. We stole the alcohol from my friend's dad's liquor supply. At thirteen years of age, I started experimenting with drugs because the alcohol was not helping. No one ever told me about Jesus that I remember. My family never went to church, prayed, or served the Lord. The drugs and alcohol led me into a life of violence, hatred, addiction, and hostility. Poverty fueled the anger I felt because of my circumstances. No one will ever convince me that God wants you to live in poverty.

Just to give you a little more background about how this revelation of Seedenomics was birthed, let me take you back to the beginning of my Christian experience. I was married at seventeen and had a child by the time I was eighteen. I took a job at the same factory where my father worked. I made $52.00 a week. I sold drugs on the side, just to be able to pay the bills. The first two years of marriage were filled with lots of anger and strife. No one could stand to be around me. My wife should have taken our son and left, but she did not. Instead, she went to church, received salvation, and began to pray for me.

I ended up in the hospital from my third overdose of drugs. I do not have space here to share my entire testimony, but it is available on my website. I will just let you know that Jesus visited me in the hospital. He told me He was going to raise me up, and I was going to carry the gospel to the world. I gave my life to Him the next day. I spent the next forty-five years trying to make up for the two years I treated my wife and child so horribly. One month and eight days after our 47th wedding anniversary, God took Ruby to heaven.

The church my late wife and I attended taught us how to scripturally support our poverty. They told us that God loved the poor and rejected the rich. We believed them, and I felt like we were the most spiritual people in the church because we were the poorest. I have come to realize that *the most dangerous doctrine is the one that supports your bondage.* These were good people who meant well— they were just deceived. I see godly people struggling today because either the culture or their church told them that it was God's will for them to be poor and that they should not seek prosperity.

Around that time, an evangelist who came to our church for a revival told us that God wanted us to prosper. I did not have a car and was walking to work. I was nineteen years old with a wife, a son, a rent payment, utilities, and groceries each week. My tithe was $5.20 because I made $52 a week.

When the evangelist came, it was late November. I had saved up $20 to buy my wife and son a little Christmas present. That was a lot of money in 1968. After he preached, the evangelist said, "I am going to receive an offering, and I want you to sow your best seed." I understood seed because I spent the summers with my grandfather who was a farmer. The evangelist went on to say, "Some of you sitting here have $20 in your pocket."

I wondered how he knew that. Something inside of me let me know I was supposed to give that $20. Sitting there, I questioned how I was going to be able to buy a Christmas present for my wife and son if I gave that money. Before I knew what was happening, I had gotten up out of my seat, walked to the front of the church, and handed the evangelist my $20. When I started back to my seat, he said, "Come here, young man." I walked back to the front, and he looked at me and said, "God told me to tell you that your ministry and your music will go around the world."

That was strange because I did not preach or sing at that time. Those words were tattooed on my spirit. I knew one day they would come to pass. As I write these words today in this book, I have written, co-written, or recorded eighty-three number one songs. Last week, we had three number one songs in one month on three different charts. I have also been on television for the last thirty-five years in over two hundred countries preaching the gospel around the world.

My seed of $20, which was all I had at that moment, birthed my destiny. Also, before I left the church that night, I had five $20 bills. The next morning, my brother who was not a believer at that time, came by my house and gave me one of his cars. You can never beat God giving.

The words of the visiting evangelist changed my life that night. He challenged me to plant a seed that would move God's hand in my life. I am eternally grateful for his instructions. My life has been one of continual seedtime and harvest since that moment. My prayer is that the words of this book will do for you what this evangelist's words did for me so many years ago. Read it with an open mind. Take notes and re-read it until it becomes part of you. *Seedtime and harvest is not an event, but a lifestyle.*

God bless you! May His best always be yours. He has given you the "*power to get wealth, that he may establish his covenant*" (Deuteronomy 8:18 KJV).

YOU ARE BLESSED TO BE A BLESSING!

Dr. James Payne
Nashville, Tennessee

Contents

PART I

SEEDENOMICS

• • • • • •

One seed sets into motion
multiplication! But it must be sown!

CHAPTER 1

Seedenomics Vs. Economics

. . . .

Hearing From the Holy Spirit

. . . .

One day, I was driving home in my pickup, praying about how to explain seedtime and harvest in a way that people could understand. I was thinking about how the revelation God had given me about finances had revolutionized my own life. I wanted the people to whom I ministered to be able to take hold of that same truth and apply it in their lives.

As I turned into my driveway, a word came up in my spirit that I had never heard before. It was the word *seedenomics*. I knew right away that this was the answer I needed. This was the way I would be able to explain the concepts of giving and receiving that were so real to me! Here was the answer—straight from the Holy Spirit!

Since then, the Holy Spirit has been teaching me and giving me new revelation daily on the difference between economics and seedenomics. I have spent numerous hours in the Word of God and have read thousands of articles on seeds. I am known throughout the world as "The Seed Man" and "The Apostle of Seedenomics." This word has become the focus and purpose of my life. I believe God has put me on this earth to help His people understand the principles of seedtime and harvest. That is why I felt compelled to write this book.

I believe the information and keys in this book will change how, when, and to what level you will prosper. When you apply these Holy Spirit-inspired principles in your life, they will bring prosperity to you and your family. Throughout this book, you will read testimonies from people just like you who have taken hold of this revelation and have begun prospering.

In the following pages, we will examine truths from God's Word, and we will uncover the deceptions and misinformation that have kept the body of Christ from prospering the way God intended. It is my prayer that this book will challenge you, empower you, and bless you. I can't wait for this revelation to spark a new level of giving in your life. Let's get started!

. . . .

A New Word for a New Mindset

. . . .

You may be asking yourself the same question that I was asking when this revelation first entered my spirit. What is *seedenomics*? We will answer this question throughout the rest of this book, but before we dive in too deeply, let's look at and define *economics*, in order to establish a foundation to compare with *seedenomics*.

Economics is a social science describing the production, distribution, and consumption of goods and services. It serves as the financial foundation of society. It's based on buying and selling, saving and investing. The study of economics deals with the relationship between supply and demand. Economics tells us that when supply is small, demand is great, and prices increase. However, when supplies are great and demand is small, prices decrease. When there is a rise in prices, there is inflation. When there is a fall in prices, there is a recession.

Those who are schooled in economics—and understand this

system—can use it to become rich and successful. Economic success is attained through human talent, education, and brainpower. Economics is driven by man's ability to cooperate and manipulate the laws of economics. Understanding trends, fads, or fashion can help individuals cash in on them and make them work in their favor.

The English word *economics* is derived from the ancient Greek word *oikomonia,* which refers to the management of a family household. Business-minded people extended it beyond the home into the world. History tells us Aristotle introduced economics around 350 BC. He described it as the study of wealth.

In the 1700s, a man named Adam Smith picked up on Aristotle's thinking and defined economics in his book *The Wealth of Nations, the Science of Wealth.*

Now let's contrast economics with the word *seedenomics.* Seedenomics is the financial foundation for the kingdom of God. It is based on seedtime and harvest. Unlike economics, which is based on science and cannot promise absolutes, seedenomics is predictable because it operates on a law given by God and on principles set in place by the teachings of Jesus. Economics is driven by man's ability; seedenomics is driven by the Holy Spirit's power.

Jesus went to great extremes to explain seedenomics in the four synoptic Gospels. He did so by speaking in parables. A parable is a simple story that illustrates a moral or spiritual lesson. Out of forty-three parables, Jesus spoke twenty-seven on seedtime and harvest. When it comes to seedenomics, most of Jesus' parables deal with agriculture.

Agri refers to farming or growing crops and raising livestock. *Culture* refers to those things that define a society such as language, lifestyle, and livelihood. When Jesus spoke these parables, agriculture made up most of the economy—which meant farming was the business of the day. Jesus spent His time speaking to farmers, so He used natural illustrations to teach spiritual revelation. He spoke in terms that farmers would understand. When His disciples asked Him why He taught the people through parables, He answered them:

Matthew 13:11 (KJV) Because it is given unto you to know the mysteries of the kingdom of heaven, but to them it is not given.

Jesus wanted this truth to be accessible to the people because they did not understand the mysteries of the kingdom. He was breaking it down for them in terms they could relate to because He wanted them to understand. He taught them through parables because He wanted seedtime and harvest to be the financial foundation for His kingdom on earth. He was not hiding these truths *from* them; He was hiding the truth *for* them.

Bird-Brained Mentality

I want to share one such lesson Jesus taught that explains the mystery of seedtime and harvest. Here is what Jesus said:

Matthew 6:24 (MSG) You can't worship two gods at once. Loving one god, you'll end up hating the other. Adoration of one feeds contempt for the other. You can't worship God and Money both.

In this text, Jesus was *not* teaching us that we should not have money; He was teaching us that money should not have us. He was making the point that money is a great servant but a poor master. Then He continues by giving us an example, showing us the difference between economics and seedenomics:

Matthew 6:25–26 (KJV) Therefore I say unto you, Take no thought for your life, what ye shall eat, or what ye shall drink; nor yet for your body, what ye shall put on. Is not the life more than meat, and the body than raiment? Behold the fowls of the air: for they sow not, neither do they reap, nor gather into barns; yet your heavenly Father feedeth them. Are ye not much better than they?

Can you imagine the setting for this teaching? Jesus had pulled away from the crowds who always followed Him and had gone up into a mountain. The disciples were all gathered around, listening to Him as He taught. The day was pleasant, the air was fresh, and there were birds busily gathering up fragments, seeds, or worms.

The crowds were never far away, though, and by positioning Himself on a steep hillside, He knew that they would be able to hear Him as they gathered below.

And He was certainly aware of what they were saying. They would be getting hungry, and the talk would inevitably turn to food. Along with the talk of food, would come the conversations about crops and herds and families and how difficult it was to make a living.

Jesus used this occasion to introduce seedtime and harvest. He began by saying, "Don't worry about food or drink or clothes." He addressed the economics that pertained to everyday life, right where people lived. They had never heard anything like this—*Don't think about how to get the things we need?* Most of the people listening probably spent most of their time thinking about the very things Jesus was talking about!

Since these are common thoughts and concerns, many individuals with religious mindsets have contemplated them throughout their lives. There are many misconceptions about the next statement that Jesus made in this discourse, when He pointed to the birds and said, "They don't plant crops or gather the harvest into barns, but your heavenly Father takes care of them."

Immediately, non-sowers develop what I call a bird-brained mentality. Here's how it is expressed: "God will take care of me; He takes care of the birds." This statement is true—if we do not mind living like a bird. Jesus was quick to point out, however, that we are better than the birds! He loves us so much and cares about us so much that He has given us the ability through seedtime and harvest to determine our own destinies financially.

Jesus was not suggesting that we just trust Him for our needs without planning, setting goals, or pursuing success. This is neither good economics nor good seedenomics. By referring to how God takes care of the birds, He was simply drawing our attention to the fact that economics alone is not the answer to meeting our needs or obtaining wealth.

Seedenomics says that what we have in our hands can be sown to bring what we need into our lives. Seedenomics will take economics, add the supernatural to it, and multiply it back to us.

Let me explain more about the concept of seedenomics with this testimony:

I was ministering in a church where a young man and his wife were pastoring. They were living in a tiny rental house close to the church with their two small children. I was invited there to teach on seedtime and harvest. At this time, the congregation was not very big, and the pastor and his wife were being paid $1,000 a month. This was $250 per week. With the obligations of the church, this was the best they could do at the time. His wife was working a job to help with the bills.

I preached that morning and told the people how I had broken the spirit of debt and moved into abundance when the Holy Spirit had led me to sow a $1,000 seed. After service, the pastor and his wife invited me to lunch. He had received his months' salary that morning. As we were eating, he signed his check and slid it across the table, saying, "I want to sow this into your ministry."

Elijah must have felt like I felt at that moment when he was taking the widow's last cake in 1 Kings 17. I knew this couple needed this more than I did. I started to say, "No, brother, you keep that," but the Holy Spirit checked me.

The pastor said, "My family and I need a home, and we can't get a loan on my salary."

This was a conclusion based on economics.

He said, "If what you taught is true, then I believe my seed will activate the supernatural, and God will make a way for us to buy a home."

I could see his faith. I prayed with them and took the check back to my office. I laid it on my desk, and I prayed for them each day. I had no intention of depositing that check. The check stayed on my desk for a week. One morning, as I reached over and laid my hand on it, I heard a voice deep inside of me say, "When are you going to deposit that seed, so I can bring in that couple's harvest?" I had just been reprimanded by my employer—God. So, I quickly deposited their check.

About six months later, this young pastor called me on a Monday. He said, "I must tell you what happened yesterday. There is a man in our church who is a builder here in our small town. He asked my wife and me to go to lunch with him and his family yesterday after church. As we were eating, he told me of a house he had built. He said that he wanted to make sure it went to the right family. He asked if we would go by and pray with him about this house. So, we agreed.

"When we pulled up to the house, my wife said, 'Oh honey, I pray one day we can have a house like this.'

"It was a beautiful home with 3 bedrooms and 2½ baths. After we toured the home, we went into the family room, joined hands, and began to pray. As the builder had requested, I prayed that the house would go to the right family. I looked up when I was finished and saw that the builder was crying.

"He looked at me and said, 'You know that morning the evangelist came to our church and spoke on seedtime and harvest?'

"I said 'Yes, that was Dr. Payne.'

"The builder said, 'That day, God told my wife and me to build you a house.'"

With that, he handed them the keys! It would have taken this couple thirty years of mortgage payments economically to get a house like this, but seedenomically, it happened in just a few months—debt-free!

This is what Jesus was trying to get His disciples—and us—to understand: He is the supernatural God who delights in doing miracles for His children. He will not overlook a seed that is sown in faith in response to the direction of the Holy Spirit. The $1,000 seed the pastor sowed into my ministry was not enough for a down payment on a home. It would not have met the need, so the young pastor made it a seed!

This is an example of seedenomics operating in the life of a believer. This is the way I have lived my life for the last thirty-four years. Here are some of the valuable insights I have learned:

- *Seedenomics is sowing as the Holy Spirit leads; it is reaping in a way that makes you a blessing.*
- *Seedenomics is not based on the world's economy; it is based on Heaven's economy.*
- *Seedenomics does not rise and fall with the stock market; it responds to seeds planted into the kingdom of God.*
- *Seedenomics does not only produce enough; it produces an overflow.*

Reading a little closer in Matthew 6, we can begin to understand that God wants us to have an abundance. Jesus points out that birds don't gather their harvest into barns. Birds don't use barns; people do!

To a farmer, a barn is a place to store their surplus. Birds live day to day and must find food daily, but Jesus is teaching us that not only can our needs be met daily, but we can also have a surplus. Just as the farmer needs a barn, He is saying that we will need a storehouse—if we practice seedtime and harvest. Last time I checked, a barn is not needed unless there is more than enough!

. . . .

Two Hundred Pennyworth

. . . .

I want to share with you another great story found in John 6. In this story, we will see Jesus illustrating the difference between economics and seedenomics. Economics is not enough to meet the need, so seedenomics is set into motion to bring in the overflow.

Jesus has been walking across the desert, stopping to preach the gospel along the way. The crowds have followed Him now for three days. This is a large crowd. Many scholars believe it numbered around fifteen thousand, counting the five thousand men and all the women and children.

They are hungry, hot, and sweaty—they are, after all, in the desert! There are no fast-food restaurants, no convenience stores, no grocery establishments from which to purchase necessities.

Jesus has been teaching for over six hours in this service, and the disciples are beginning to survey the situation. I can hear Peter saying, "You know I love to hear Jesus speak, but He has been at this for a long time, now. Someone needs to go tell Him it's time to wrap it up so these people can go home.

The disciples are getting concerned and decide that someone has to talk with Jesus. They choose Philip as their designated spokesman. This is how the conversation with Jesus goes for Philip:

> *John 6:5–7 (KJV). When Jesus then lifted up his eyes and saw a great company come unto him, he saith unto Philip, Whence shall we buy bread, that these may eat? And this he said to prove him: for he himself knew what he would do. Philip answered him, Two hundred pennyworth of bread is not sufficient for them, that every one of them may take a little.*

Jesus acknowledged that there was a need, so He asked Philip, "Where will we buy bread so all these people can eat?" Notice this disciple's response.

You know the disciples. They were just ordinary fishermen, tax collectors, and common citizens until Jesus plucked them from obscurity and placed them into the spotlight. They now have celebrity status. They are the Jesus posse! They are His ministry team. They have spent time in the ministry of Jesus as He performed miracles to crowds of thousands. They are on stage with a man who is opening blind eyes, making the lame to walk, causing the deaf to hear, and even raising the dead back to life.

Now, they find themselves in a position where Jesus is trying their faith. He is asking a question that He knows will be answered based on economics.

Questions ran through Philip's mind. *Where will we buy bread? Do we have any food on hand? It's been three days—whatever we had with us is long gone.* Philip finally answered, "We only have two hundred pennyworth of bread, and that is not enough."

Don't you believe Jesus already knew that this was not going to be enough? Of course! This was a teachable moment. Jesus knew that what was in their possession economically was not enough to meet their needs. Even if there had been places to buy food, they still wouldn't have had enough money among them to buy that much bread.

Today, Jesus will teach them about seedenomics. He intends to teach them that the kingdom in which they have enlisted to serve is different. He is there to provide them with the tools they will need to birth the church and establish the kingdom of God. He knows He only has a short time before He goes to Calvary and back to Heaven. The text said that Jesus already knew what He planned to do! He always knows what *He* will do; He wants to know what *we* will do.

. . . .

Twelve Baskets Full

. . . .

Philip has inventoried the available food and found that there is nothing available except five loaves and two fish from a young lad's lunch. Philip said, "What good will that do us?

Economics is not enough to provide for the need that is in front of them at this time. However, Philip is about to give the young man an opportunity to go from economics to seedenomics. He is giving this lad an opportunity to sow a seed into the ministry of Jesus.

One thing about this miracle always bothered me until the Lord began to reveal something to me about the lad with the five loaves and two fish. This lad was a businessman!

Having been to Israel, I want to point out something that I have noticed, and that I believe has bearing on what happened in this story. Children in Israel are often entrepreneurs. They find a crowd and then work that crowd, selling postcards, pictures, water, souvenirs, or whatever they have. I believe the lad who had five loaves and two fish was there selling food to the crowd. I believe he had started the morning with twelve full baskets. He likely had some type of wagon or cart, and he loaded those baskets that morning and followed the crowd. He was almost sold out when Philip presented him with the opportunity to sow what he had left into the ministry of Jesus!

Now, I realize I don't have any scripture to prove my interpretation of this story, but no one else has any proof that it *didn't* happen this way! How else would you notice a kid in a crowd of fifteen thousand if he were not doing something that made him stand out? I can imagine him proclaiming rather loudly, "Fishes and loaves, fishes and loaves!"

As we read on in this story, we find that this lad made the best decision of his life by giving Jesus what he had left. He was practicing economics, and Jesus was going to reveal to him the principle of seedenomics.

Jesus goes into action. He tells His disciples to have the people sit down in companies of fifty. He then takes the loaves and fish and gives thanks. Then, He begins to break the bread and fish into pieces— and as He does, it multiplies.

It has been estimated that during this time a woman would eat one-third of a loaf of bread. Men would consume two-thirds of a loaf of bread. Women would eat one fish and men would eat two fish at a setting. If you were to multiply these numbers, you would see that it would have taken over five thousand loaves to feed this crowd. It would also have taken between fifteen and twenty thousand fish. This equates to nearly one and a half semi-trucks full of food that Jesus produced to feed this crowd.

The crowds, the disciples, and now those of us who are reading this account are being taught that this is not just a kid's lunch— this is a seed that has found its way into the hands of Jesus. Everything that gets into the hands of Jesus multiplies! He breaks off a fish head and another appears. He breaks a loaf, and it is whole again. It's supernatural. This is seedenomics. The seeds we place into Jesus' hands are multiplied and will bring increase into our lives.

Jesus took what was tangible or natural and added the supernatural. He took what He was given and multiplied it. One thing I do know for a fact is that I have never given anything to Jesus that He didn't multiply and give back to me in a greater measure than I gave. This young man learned this lesson. After everyone had been fed, the young man had his twelve baskets back—and they were all full! What he gave Jesus became a seed that took the young man from economics into seedenomics.

In this story, we can see two different mindsets. One reflected how *Philip* thought; the other reflected how *Jesus* thought. Philip suggested to Jesus that two hundred pennyworth of bread (economics) was not enough to give everyone even a little! Jesus, however, gave everyone enough to fill them up and have twelve baskets full leftover (seedenomics).

Today, we either serve this same Jesus, or we don't. He either can do what He once did, or He cannot. I choose to believe that this same Jesus who multiplied the loaves and fish is the same Jesus who multiplies the seeds we sow into kingdom work. This is the seedenomics mentality. *God can take the seed we sow and produce the harvest that we need.*

· · · · · · · · · · · · · ·

Seedenomics Can Manipulate Economics

· · · · · · · · · · · · · ·

There was a real estate broker who heard me preach on this story from Matthew 6. Her company was going under. She was preparing to close her office, and she was telling her agents to find other employment. That morning, I received an offering to help defray the expenses of installing some much-needed equipment in that local church.

The broker wrote to me a few weeks later. She had sown a sacrificial seed that morning for her company. Shortly after she sowed her seed, everyone in the company began to sell properties that had been sitting idle for weeks. She told me that it was her seed that had turned the company around!

Was this a coincidence? Ask yourself: Was it a coincidence that there was a lad where Jesus was preaching with just what Jesus needed for a miracle? I believe seedenomics was in operation! Seedenomics can turn a business, a church, a city, a town, or even a country around. *Seedenomics can manipulate economics.*

For us to prosper, we must develop a seedenomics mindset. Our mindset will either attract the prosperity of the Lord, or it will repel it. The Word of God must be the final authority regarding riches, wealth, blessing, increase, and prosperity in our lives. When we entertain negative thoughts that oppose the Word of God, it opens the door to unbelief, doubt, and fear. I want to help you build a seedenomics mindset.

Things To Remember From Chapter One:

1. *Economics is the financial foundation of society. Seedenomics is the financial foundation of the kingdom of God.*

2. *Economics is driven by human power. Seedenomics is driven by Holy Spirit power.*

3. *Seedenomics says that what we have in our hands can be sown to bring about what we need in our lives.*

4. *Seedenomics can manipulate economics.*

5. *Seedenomics is a prosperity mindset, not a poverty mindset.*

6. *Seedenomics is where the supernatural meets economics.*

7. *Seedenomics doesn't produce just enough, it produces an overflow.*

CHAPTER 2

The Creation of the Seed

The only place HARVEST comes before
SEEDTIME is in the dictionary!

. . . .

Light and Lineage

. . . .

Let there be light! The earth lay in chaos for millions of years; darkness covered the face of the deep. Suddenly, the Spirit of God began to move back and forth over the waters of the earth. God spoke, and His Word ricocheted from the mountains to the valleys. All Heaven stood at attention and the earth opened its ears as the voice of the Creator said, "Let there be light!" At 186,000 miles per second, light began to travel, creating as it moved, galaxy after galaxy until the universe became too large to measure.

The Divine Creator struck the anvil of His omnipotence with the steel hammer of His omnipresence, caught the sparks on His fingertips and tossed them into the darkness. The stars appeared as diamonds displayed on black velvet. This was the first performance of the God who is more than enough. Dividing light from darkness, morning from evening, He marked His calendar as the **FIRST DAY!**

God continued speaking, causing the division of land and sea. The waters were held back, and the dry ground appeared, in preparation for a seed not yet created. The firmament was formed— the solid dome of earth called Heaven, which would allow the waters to recirculate and nourish the earth. This was the **SECOND DAY!**

These first two days of creation produced the first essential elements necessary for seedtime and harvest–first light, then ground, then water.

The third day was a natural illustration of a great spiritual truth. The third day was the centerpiece for revelation. On the third day, on the third planet from the sun, God created the seed. And once God created the seed, He never created it again. Every seed traces its lineage back to the **THIRD DAY!**

. . . .

Why Did God Create The Seed?

. . . .

God created the seed for provision. He knew humanity would need a means of sustenance. He created a garden that contained trees to feed humanity. The fruit of the trees contained seeds to bring forth harvests of plenty for future generations:

> *Genesis 2:8 (KJV) God planted seed and caused the earth to bring forth.*

God created seeds and, in each seed, He not only spoke multiplication, but He also spoke destiny. The destiny of every seed is to multiply and produce a harvest. He spoke destiny to every seed and gave every seed an assignment. He put three functions in every seed:

➢ *To Die*
➢ *To Resurrect*
➢ *To Multiply*

. . . .

The Seed's First Function: to Die

. . . .

John 12:24 (KJV) Verily, verily, I say unto you, Except a corn of wheat fall into the ground and die, it abideth alone: but if it die, it bringeth forth much fruit.

The first thing a seed was created to do is **die**. Jesus used a corn, or what we would today call a kernel, of wheat to introduce and describe His death, burial, and resurrection. A corn of wheat is a seed that still has the outward husk on the seed. Jesus used this to let us know it was His flesh—the outward body—that would be transformed by His death and resurrection. Like a natural seed, He would not die in the sense of ceasing to live, but in the sense of transforming from one state of existence to another.

When a seed enters the soil, it loses its identity and dies. It becomes invisible to the natural eye. The seed is no longer under the control of the sower. The word *die* here does not mean *to cease to exist*, it means *to transform into a new form of life*.

The seed was created to die and be buried so that it could come forth as a new creation. That new creation was in the seed the whole time. It just needed to be planted and connected with the soil so it could resurrect.

The natural always mirrors the spiritual. Just like a seed, we must die to ourselves, be transformed, take on the identity of Christ, and fulfill our destiny on this earth.

. . . .

The Seed's Second Function: to Resurrect

. . . .

The second ability a seed has is to **resurrect**. To resurrect means to restore or bring back to life. The moment a seed dies, a metamorphosis begins to take place. What once was a seed when it entered the soil, dies, resurrects, and comes back as a harvest. I would like to share with you how this process takes place.

Initially, the seed makes a connection with the soil. When the seed is planted into the soil, the earth begins to vibrate. As the soil begins to vibrate, the seventeen essential nutrients in the soil that the growing plant will need begin to make their way to the seed.

God had the foresight to put into the soil all the nutrients the seed would need in order to produce a harvest.

Out of the seventeen nutrients, three specific nutrients play a key role in the harvest: nitrogen, phosphorus, and potassium. It is these three nutrients that meet and ignite the seed—activating it and setting things into motion. The nutrients in the soil ignite the seed making it ready for multiplication. In the same way, the nutrients in the soil when you sow your seed ignite it for a harvest in the spirit realm.

Once the nutrients ignite the seed, the process of growth begins in several different areas of the seed:

The seed coat: The seed begins to shed its hard protective shell called the *seed coat*. The seed coat is what protects the seed from harm—from physical damage, temperature-related damage, or water damage. This outer shell also protects the seed from parasites. Once the outer shell is shed, water begins to fill the seed.

The water activates enzymes that begin plant growth. The "water" of the Word of God (see Ephesians 5:26) is a type of the Spirit of God. When the Spirit permeates your seed, it will also initiate growth.

The endosperm: The endosperm stores a supply of nutrients and provides them to the heart of the seed. The endosperm also responds to the environment around it and regulates the growth of the new plant.

The embryo: The embryo is the heart of the seed. The embryo is the part of the seed where the earliest forms of the roots, stems, leaves, and other organs are formed.

The radicle: Once the seed begins to grow, within 24-48 hours it develops what is called a *radicle*. The radicle is the primary root, which is the first thing to emerge from the seed. The radicle anchors the plant to the ground by growing downward and allowing it to absorb water. This process is called *germination*.

The shoot: After the root absorbs the water, the *shoot* emerges from the seed and pushes its way up through the soil. This process is called *emergence*. Once the shoot breaks through the ground, it grows toward the sun. Once the new growth is hit by the light, emergence gives way to *multiplication*.

. . . .

The Seed's Third Function: to Multiply

. . . .

The third ability a seed has is the ability to **multiply**. The multiplication of seed is what gives it the ability to produce exponentially. In the natural, once a seed begins to multiply, it does not stop. In the spiritual, the seeds you sow into the kingdom do not stop producing unless you stop sowing. The law of multiplication only stops when the seed stops. That is why it is important to keep on sowing. The moment you continue to sow seed, the continuation of multiplication operates in that seed.

Let me demonstrate the power of multiplication in the seed:

➤ Each apple has an average of 6 seeds.
➤ These seeds can grow 6 trees.
➤ Each tree can produce about 300 apples.
➤ Six trees can produce a total of 1800 apples.
➤ There are six seeds in each of those 1800 apples.
➤ Now you have 10,800 seeds.
➤ Those 10,800 seeds can produce 10,800 trees.
➤ Each tree can produce about 300 apples.
➤ You have a total of 3,240,000 apples.

➢ Each of those apples has 6 seeds.
➢ Now you have 19,440,000 seeds!

This is the demonstration of seedenomics. Every seed—whether it's an apple or a dollar bill—can multiply dramatically, given the right circumstances and environment!

This example shows us a powerful revelation: ***there is a harvest in every seed and a seed in every harvest.*** If you take the seed that you reaped and replant it, then you will reap perpetual blessings. Sowing seed is not a one-time event; it is a lifestyle. I want to share with you a story that I read some time back about a man who experienced seed multiplication firsthand in his life.

. . . .

Johnny Appleseed

. . . .

John Chapman, better known as Johnny Appleseed, lived in the 1800s. Johnny lived with meager means and traveled throughout the country as an evangelist. He was known to be a humble man with no frills. He wore the same clothes every day, and he did not wear any shoes. He would stay with people everywhere he went to speak. As a means of raising money for his traveling expenses, he planted apple seeds. These apple seeds would grow into apple trees.

It sounds unusual until you hear *why* he planted those apple seeds: he planted for a harvest. Not only did he plant apple seeds to help his ministry, but he also planted apple seeds because there was a law in place that said if you planted fifty apple trees on a piece of land, you became the owner of that land. So, Johnny Appleseed planted seeds everywhere he went. He reaped a harvest of both apple trees and land ownership.

His harvest gave him ownership that no one could take from him and his family. He was instrumental in introducing apple trees to large parts of Pennsylvania, Ohio, Indiana, Illinois, and Ontario, Canada.

During his lifetime, it is said that Johnny Appleseed planted two million seeds and became the owner of 1200 acres of property. His harvest outlived him. The oldest tree he planted is said to still be producing apples at 178 years old. If Johnny were here with us today, I believe he would say, "Don't ever stop planting seeds because what you sow will multiply!"

. . . .

Destiny In The Seed

. . . .

Within the seed that God created on the third day, there are not only abilities but also destiny. When God created seed, **He programmed every seed to know its destiny.** Every seed came with an instruction, a spoken word from the mouth of God. He spoke destiny to the seed and put in it the DNA to reproduce after its own kind:

> *Genesis 1:11 (KJV) God said, Let the earth bring forth grass, the herb yielding seed, and the fruit tree yielding fruit after his kind, whose seed is in itself, upon the earth: and it was so. And the earth brought forth grass, and herb yielding seed after his kind, and the tree yielding fruit, whose seed was in itself, after his kind: and God saw that it was good. And the evening and the morning were the third day.*

This means He made the tomato seed to produce tomatoes. He made the corn seed to produce corn. A corn seed does not have to *try* to produce corn, its DNA is *designed* to produce corn. When you hold a grain of corn in your hand, that one seed goes back to the third day of creation. He made the watermelon seed to produce watermelons. He made the apple seed to produce apples. He made the money seed to produce money. Which tells me that if I want corn, I sow corn. If I want watermelons, I sow watermelons. If I want apples, I sow apples. If I want money, I sow money.

Now, in the spiritual, it's also true that every seed produces after its kind. If I want mercy, I sow mercy. If I want grace, I sow grace. If I want power, I sow prayer because prayer will produce the power I need to be victorious. If I want a revelation, I sow studying because the mysteries of Christ are revealed to me when I seek God through His Holy Scriptures.

Another truth is that the size of the harvest I want to reap must be reflected by the size of seed I am willing to sow. The size of my harvest will be determined by the size of my seed.

Fruit forms around the seed. The aroma of the fruit is released when the seed is exposed. If you cut open an apple or a peach, you will see the seed. Even blindfolded, you can identify the fruit by the smell. The fruit or the harvest that you need from God will form around the seed that you sow into His work and His kingdom.

> *2 Corinthians 9:6-7 (ASV) But this I say, He that soweth sparingly shall reap also sparingly; and he that soweth bountifully shall also reap bountifully. Let each man do according as he hath purposed in his heart: not grudgingly, or of necessity: for God loveth a cheerful giver.*

This is not talking about the quantity of the seed; it is dealing with the quality of the seed. If a seed is not planted from a place of sacrifice or obedience to the Holy Spirit, that seed will not be able to bring forth its full harvest.

Let me explain it like this to you: *if I continue to sow what I do not need, I will continue to reap what I cannot use.* If the seeds you have been sowing are out of convenience, don't be surprised when you reap little. I learned a long time ago in my own life that seeds which were sown in comfort would be reaped in mediocrity.

If I want a different harvest, I must sow a different type of seed—such as seeds I'd rather keep, bigger seeds, and seeds that stretch my faith. When I sow seeds that I would rather keep, it causes God to release what He never intended to keep from me. Believe me when I tell you that I sowed my way out of poverty, lack, and want. I sowed my way out of debt, and I sowed my way into abundance. I know the same thing can happen to you when you start activating seedenomics in your life.

. . . .

God Is The Lord Of The Harvest
Man Is The Lord Of The Seed

. . . .

When God created the seed, He had man in mind. The Bible says that when God created Adam, He made him the caretaker of the seed. He left the destiny of the seed in his hands. He created Adam from the dust of *the earth*, breathed life in him, and gave him dominion.

> *Genesis 1:26 (KJV) God said, "Let Us make man in Our image, according to Our likeness; let them have dominion over the fish of the sea, over the birds of the air, and over the cattle, over all the earth and over every creeping thing that creeps on the earth."*

When God gave Adam dominion, it included the responsibility of, choosing the soil, tilling the ground, weeding the field, and bringing in the harvest.

This tells us that He made man the Lord of the Seed. *God is the Lord of the harvest, but He made man the lord of the seed.* When He gave man dominion, He gave man a choice. God said, "I created the seed to produce what I promised. Now what you do with that seed is in your hands."

Note what is being conveyed here: the power of multiplication is *in the seed*, but the decision to sow the seed is *in your hands*. When God created the seed, He put destiny in the seed, but gave the man the choice to plant that seed. He was saying, 'Adam, you can eat all the seed, or you can sow a portion of it."

After Adam was created, God put him to sleep and took a rib from his side that He used to create Eve, a helpmate who would assist him as caretaker of the seed. Then Satan came to the garden as a snake, and sin entered the human race because Adam and Eve disobeyed a command from the Lord.

When God created the seed, it was not just for eating—it was also for sowing. Seed needs to be sown—the multiplication and destiny in each seed are only activated when it is sown. If we were to quit sowing seeds, we would create a deficit of resources needed to sustain future generations.

For example, if every farmer on earth were to eat every seed that was harvested, then starvation would occur around the world. Our economic system, horticultural system, and financial system depend on the planting of seeds. The greatest minds of the world know this is true. In fact, there is already a plan in place to safeguard seeds for future generations.

. . . .

Seed Vault

. . . .

In Norway, there is a seed vault that cost nine million dollars to build, plus many millions more to maintain. It is commonly called the Doomsday Vault. It is situated well back into the side of a mountain. It has a storage capacity of 4.5 million seed samples, with each sample containing five hundred seeds on average. At last count, it contained well over a million different varieties of seeds. The builders say that if there is an apocalyptic event, the seeds that are stored in this vault can restore society.

It is reported that over 1,750 seed vaults exist in the world. When one country invades another, one of the first actions of the military is often to destroy their seed bank. This is a military tactic that has been used for years. Satan uses the same strategy today. If he can destroy your seed, he can ensure your destruction. Without seed, there can be no harvest!

Seeds are one of the most precious commodities that we possess. We must protect this foundation as a stable source for years to come. We have certainly learned this over the last few years. The recent pandemic of the Covid 19 virus that hit the world caused the sale of seeds to soar in America.

When people began to see empty grocery store shelves, they began to realize the source of their food. People are returning to backyard gardens, canning, and storing the harvest. The fundamental basics that all societies are built on are *sowing* and *reaping, seedtime* and *harvest*. We must get back to sowing. We must learn to sow what we have, to create what we need.

. . . .

Redemption Seed

. . . .

Everything that happens in the natural is mirrored in the supernatural. God created seed for man, but man sinned. Man ate the seed that he was not supposed to partake of from the tree. God knew this would happen, so He already had a plan in place for redemption.

The plan involved a seed named Jesus. The Bible tells *us that Christ was a seed (see Galatians 3:16 NKJV).* The seed of God was planted in a virgin named Mary, and she brought forth a son named Jesus. He was the seed of God and the Son of God. This Son would be the seed that would bring forth a harvest of children for God. God had a son, but Jesus would give Him a family.

Every human, saved or lost, is the seed of God. This is the reason man is drawn toward the things of God. Some respond and some reject the drawing of the Lord. The only true happiness a person ever finds is in making Jesus the Lord of their life and living under the leadership of the Holy Spirit. This is priceless!

Man's first classroom was a garden, and his first lesson was on seed. It was here God introduced His son (His seed).

> *Genesis 3:15 (KJV) And I will put enmity between thee and the woman, and between thy seed and her seed; it shall bruise they head, and thou shalt bruise his heel.*

The word enmity is used for warfare. God was announcing a battle that would occur between His seed and Satan's seed.

When God created the seed, He knew man would sin, and He would have to redeem man with a seed. This seed would have to be planted in a garden. Because sin began in a garden, Jesus would be crucified for sin in a garden. The seed, Jesus, was hung on a tree in a place called Calvary. The tree on which He died grew from a seed that had been planted and led back to the third day of creation.

Eve was taken from Adam's side to be his wife; through the water and blood spilled from the side of Jesus by a Roman spear, God brought forth the bride of Christ—the church.

God planted His only begotten son as a seed so that we might have eternal life. The seed died and was planted in a garden in a borrowed tomb.

> *John 19:41 (NKJV) Now in the place where He was crucified there was a garden, and in the garden a new tomb in which no one had yet been laid.*

Just like a natural seed is buried, the spiritual seed was buried. A seed must be buried in order to experience a resurrection. Then, on the third day, the stone was rolled away. The seed emerged from the tomb.

He went into the tomb a seed; He came out as a Savior. He went into the tomb where all His power was ignited. He arose with healing in His wings. He became the seed so that we could experience redemption. God knew that man would need to be redeemed with a seed. Jesus became that seed. That seed goes back to the third day of creation and changed all humanity on another third day.

Things To Remember From Chapter Two:

1. *Seed was created on the third day with three distinct functions: to die, to resurrect, and to multiply.*

2. *God's Word is in every seed.*

3. *God only created seed one time.*

4. *God is Lord of the harvest; man is lord of the seed.*

5. *Seed was created to produce after its own kind.*

6. *We determine the size of our harvest by the size of the seed we sow.*

7. *God's seed Jesus was planted for our redemption. Jesus went into the tomb a seed and came out a Savior.*

CHAPTER 3

The Gospel According to a Seed Packet

Missing an opportunity is the most expensive mistake you will ever make.

The revelation of seedtime and harvest began for me at my local hardware store. At that time, I lived on a farm with forty acres of property, so I planted a garden every year. One year, I was in the store looking at the seed display, and I felt the Lord begin to speak to me. I was holding packages of corn, tomatoes, watermelons, cucumbers, and carrots in my hand. The Lord said, "What do you have?"

I looked down at the package of corn, which had a picture on the front. I said, "Corn."

The Lord said, "That is not corn—that is only a picture of corn." Immediately, He had my attention. He said, "My children only have a picture of what they can have; they do not have the product. You have a picture of corn, but you do not have corn. For the picture to become a reality, you must sow the seed that will create the product."

This was a simple yet profound revelation. The picture let me know that the seed had the ability to call things that are not as though they already were. The picture was a result of someone sowing a seed and that seed producing the product that gave the photographer the corn to photograph.

So many times, people walk through the grocery store isles and never realize that someone planted the tomatoes they are purchasing. Those same people sit in church, hear the music, and listen to the preaching without ever realizing someone planted seeds to build the building, purchase the seats, turn on the heat and air, buy the sound equipment, and pay the salaries of the church staff. This is the reason Jesus taught seedtime and harvest as the economic foundation for the church and the kingdom of God.

I want to share with you in this chapter the five truths that I learned from a package of seeds. This revelation has changed my life, and I know that it will change your life—and your family's life—when you apply it.

. . . .

First Truth: People Sow According To Their Appetite

. . . .

Standing at the seed display that day, I was holding corn, tomatoes, watermelons, cucumbers, and carrots. Those are the products I love. I was not holding okra because I am not a fan. I was holding what I had an appetite for in my life. I understood that because seeds produce after their own kind, I would not sow corn and reap okra. You must sow according to your appetite.

In the financial realm, the same thing is true. You sow according to your appetite. If you love cars, you sow for cars. If a house is your priority, you sow for a house. Some people love to travel, so they sow to travel. Someone else loves the work of God, and their appetite is to sow as often as they can, and as much as they can to help the church or missions.

When I was growing up, my mom had an appetite for tomatoes. She would sow several different types of tomatoes each year. She used those tomatoes for soup, sauces, and other dishes. My life until I left home was seeing her plant and can tomatoes every year to use during the winter months. She sowed according to her appetite.

Just as my mom planted what *she* had an appetite for, *we* can assess what we have an appetite for in our lives. For example, you can look at your bank statement and tell what you have an appetite for in your life. Your spending habits will testify to your appetite. If you are not happy with your current situation, you must change your appetite.

This is the place I found myself in a little over thirty-five years ago. I was over one million dollars in debt. I got to that place with an appetite for boats, sports cars, houses I could not afford, and a lifestyle that required me to charge a lot of the things that I purchased. I was buying things I could not afford, with money I did not have, to impress people I didn't even know. I had to change my appetite.

I wanted things to change, so I developed an appetite to get out of debt. I was able to sell everything, pay everyone, and live debt-free for the last thirty-four years. Debt-free sure tastes better than debt. I changed my appetite, and with God's help, you can do the same in your life.

. . . .

Second Truth: Every Seed Packet Has a Prophecy on the Front of the Package

. . . .

The prophecy on the front of each package tells you how long it will take to receive your harvest after you plant the seed. Tomatoes—80 days. Corn—65 to 70 days. Cucumbers—55 days. Watermelons—80 to 90 days, depending on the type. Every seed is programmed for a harvest, but the time between the sowing of your seed and the reaping of your harvest can seem like an eternity.

In the spiritual realm, we can see this explained in the scriptures:

Galatians 6:9 (KJV) And let us not be weary in well doing: for in due season, we shall reap if we faint not.

The same thing is true in the spiritual realm that is true in the natural. You will reap what you sow. The only difference is that the timing is different in the spiritual realm. People who have sown corn, tomatoes, cucumbers, and watermelons know how long it takes to get a harvest. The sellers of the seed can accurately predict the time of the harvest.

What amazes me is that although people don't know the manufacturer of the seed packet, they believe what is written on the package. The same people know Jesus, but do not believe what is written in his Word about seedtime and harvest.

In the spiritual realm, however, there is no prophetic word that says you will have a harvest in a certain number of days. The promise is we shall reap *in due season.*

When we sow a financial seed, immediately the devil will start working on our minds telling us we will never get a harvest. Well, the devil is a liar (John 8:44 KJV).

Don't believe what the enemy says—focus on what God said: *In due season, we shall reap…IF WE FAINT NOT!* These four words tell us that it is possible to sow and miss our harvest if we faint. To *faint* means to give in to impatience, fear, doubt, unbelief, and other adverse circumstances.

When a natural seed is sown, it attracts the nutrients in the earth that cause it to germinate. Then, when the bloom comes on the plant, it attracts bees, bats, and birds that pollinate the plant.

This also works in the financial realm, when we sow a seed into the kingdom of God, and God's work. Our seed attracts God's attention, and God sets into motion our financial harvest. We begin to walk in favor. The boss who would never give us a raise suddenly calls us into the office and increases our income. The property that we need to sell—that no one has even looked at—begins to attract potential buyers. The business that is failing now succeeds. This is seedenomics in action.

. . . .

Third Truth: The Seed Packet Tells You The Proper Season To Sow

. . . .

On the back of every seed packet in America, there is a color-coded map that defines your window of opportunity. This is the time when you should sow. If you miss this moment, you must wait another year. You must ask yourself: can you wait another year?

The same is true in the area of finance. God will speak to us either personally or through one of His servants. One day, while I was recovering from the COVID-19 virus—from which I almost died twice during the twenty-seven days I battled the virus, I was watching a ministry service on television. In the midst of this battle, God impressed upon me while the minister was speaking that I was to sow a seed. So, I went online and obeyed the Lord promptly.

Had I waited, I could have missed this moment and missed a blessing from the Lord. It was my window, my moment of opportunity created by the voice of the Holy Spirit. When God is talking to you about a seed, He has a harvest that He wants to send to your life.

Ecclesiastes 3:1-2 (KJV) *To every thing there is a season, and a time to every purpose under the heaven: A time to be born, and a time to die; a time to plant, and a time to pluck up that which is planted.*

The word *time* in this text means a window of opportunity created by a Word from God. It may be a moment, a day, a month, or a year. The longer you delay your obedience to sow, the longer you delay your harvest! *It is better to give in the opportunity of the moment than it is to miss the moment of opportunity.* There are some things we need to know about *opportunity*:

A. *Opportunity knocks on everyone's door:* When we need a harvest, God will create an opportunity for us to sow. I don't schedule any meetings in December. Churches are busy with other things, and they do not schedule many guests.

This past year, I was praying about my budget for December, and God created an opportunity for me to sow. I was on a mission trip in another country, and God spoke to me about sowing a $10,000 seed. It was not a *good* time, but it was a *God* time. Not all seeds are easy to sow. I quickly obeyed the Lord, and He not only met my budget for December, but He also met it for the following year—within six days after I sowed that seed!

You may feel as though you have missed a great harvest in your life because you were not obedient to the prompting of God concerning sowing. You can change that today. Make up your mind that you will never miss another window of opportunity!

B. *When opportunity knocks, don't allow fear to answer the door!* When I was nineteen years old, I was called to preach. There had never been a preacher in our family. One night, my pastor asked me to preach the following Sunday. I was scared to death. I couldn't sleep; I couldn't eat. This was my first opportunity to preach. I was also supposed to play my guitar and sing before I preached. There would only be about one hundred and fifty or so people present in the service.

Sunday came, and I wanted to call in sick. Instead, I faced my fears. The song and the sermon were not all that great! Had I let fear answer the door of opportunity, my ministry would not be where it is today. I have preached on television to millions since that time.

C. Missing a moment of opportunity will be the most expensive mistake you will ever make. A few years back, I was raising money to get a church out of foreclosure! I challenged people to sow a $1,000 seed. Several people responded, including me, and we were able to get the church caught up on their payments. Their seed began to cause a parade of miracles.

One year later, I went back to burn the church mortgage. When I got there, a man walked up to me and told me a story.

He said, "When you were here a year ago, my business was going under. I was about to lose everything. It was a challenge to sow a $1,000 seed that morning when you asked us to sow for the church. After my wife and I obeyed, a man from an oil company stopped by our house and asked permission to drill on our property. They found a rich deposit of natural gas. My first tithe check was $50,000."

Several other people who gave that morning had the same results. One young couple that I know was able to build their dream home and pay cash for it. Another man walked up to me, and he was truly angry—but not at me.

He said, "The morning you were here and asked people to give $1,000, I told the Lord that I could not do it. My farm was in foreclosure. A few weeks after you were here, they sold my farm on the courthouse steps, and a friend of mine bought it.

"A few weeks after he bought it, they found the richest deposit of natural gas in this area on what used to be my farm. I drive by there every day on the way to our small rental house, and I hear your voice every time I do. I hear you saying that if you will obey God with a $1,000 seed, He can turn your financial situation around."

He said, "If I had only listened..."

How many times have we missed our harvest because we missed our window of opportunity? It is the most expensive mistake we will ever make.

. . . .

Fourth Truth: The Seed Can Call Things That Be Not As Though They Already Were

. . . .

Look at a package of seeds. There is always a four-color picture of the product that the seed is going to produce. To have the product, you must open the package and plant the seed. Each day, calling things that be not as though they were starts bringing this picture into reality. For instance, when you sow corn, it brings forth a stalk.

On that stalk, two ears of corn appear. Each ear of corn has approximately seven hundred and fifty kernels. One seed turns into 1500 seeds. If we plant those seeds one more time, it will produce 2,250,000 seeds. This is God's law of multiplication of the seed to the third power.

If what we have financially is not enough, we should plant it. Every penny of money that comes through our hands must be handled like a seed that comes to a farmer. Our seed predicts our future. It takes a *right-now seed*, to produce a *not-yet harvest*.

> *Heb. 11:1 (KJV) Now faith is the substance of things hoped for, the evidence of things not seen.*

The entire eleventh chapter of Hebrews deals with things not seen. By faith, Noah built an ark when he had never seen rain. By faith, Abraham left his homeland and family even though he had never seen the Promised Land.

> *2 Corinthians 5:7 (KJV) For we walk by faith and not by sight.*

What we cannot see is greater than what we can see. We cannot be moved by what we can see. It's okay to talk about things that are unseen. After all, the seed packet has a picture of the product you will harvest.

. . . .

A Picture of Debt-Free

. . . .

Years ago, when I was in debt and thought I could never get out, I came up with a plan. I figured up how much money I would need to pay off all my creditors. Then, I wrote a check for that amount. I did not sign the check, but I laminated it and put it in my Bible as a bookmark in Hebrews 11. I would look at it every day. That check, like the seed packet, was calling things that be not as though they already were. I would look at the check, and I would plant seeds and write on my check, "Breaking the spirit of debt." Twelve months later, I was debt-free, and I have been since that day. Get a picture you can focus on in your mind until the harvest arrives.

. . . .

Fifth Truth: The Seed Has An Assignment

. . . .

God named the seeds He created, and their names defined their assignments. The assignment for a tomato seed is to produce tomatoes. The assignment for a cucumber seed is to produce cucumbers. Tomatoes and cucumbers don't have to try to become tomatoes and cucumbers—it is their assignment!

God spoke their destiny and prophesied their future the day He created them. Scientists cannot create a seed. The seed fulfills its assignment because God spoke His Word over the seed and told it to multiply. The same thing is true when we speak over our seeds.

If the seeds remain in the package, they will never fulfill their assignment. Everyone who knows me knows that I always carry packets of seeds around with me. Some of those packets are seven years old. They have never produced a harvest because I hold their destiny in my hand. I have a peach seed that I carry in my pocket next to my money clip that is twenty-six years old. It has never produced a peach. I have contained its destiny for the last twenty-six years. Had I sown it, I could have had an orchard by now.

This is the reason we must give our financial seeds an assignment when we sow them. Some people get confused when you say this. They say, "Well, you can't buy a miracle. That type of thinking can keep you from getting a miracle. No person in their right mind would think you can buy a miracle!

When you give your seed an assignment, you are doing what God did when He created seeds. He gave them names, and He gave them an assignment. When you sow a financial seed, you need to name that seed and give that seed an assignment.

A couple I know, after hearing me preach several times through the years, told me this story. They had been trying to sell their house for over a year; they wanted to move and build a new house. Not one person had looked at their home. The real estate agents were telling them they were asking too much for the property. At lunch one Sunday after church, the lady said to her husband, "Why don't we sow a seed for the sale of our house—and give it an assignment."

This was at 1 p.m. They sowed a $1,000 seed! They named the seed: "This seed is for the sale of our home." They gave that seed an assignment. They prayed to let someone drive by and know that this was the house for them. At 3 p.m. that same afternoon, someone drove by, saw the sign in the yard, called them, and offered them a full-price offer. Some people would say this is a coincidence. I don't believe that. I believe their act of faith in sowing the seed set things in motion for the sale of the home.

What happened for that couple can happen for you. If you need a job, a raise, a car, a home, ministry doors to open, a family loved one to be saved, a marriage to be healed, or any other need—sow a seed! Name that seed. Give that seed an assignment. Water that seed with your praise. Protect your heart from the weeds that Satan tries to sow. Call things that be not as though they were, just like the picture on the front of that seed packet calls that picture into a product. Give your seed an assignment and wait with expectation for your due season.

After serving God for forty-six years in full-time ministry and sowing thousands of dollars into His work, I have developed an expectancy from sowing that makes my harvest almost instant. Let me give you an example.

In one special service, God spoke to me to sow $5,000 to help a fellow minister celebrate fifty years of ministry. I sowed my seed with many other believers. Before I left the building, a man walked up to me. He said, "When I passed you in the hall of the hotel this morning, God told me to give you this." He handed me a check for $5,000. I had my seed back. As I held his hand and prayed over his seed, people gathered and began to hand me money. My blessing came before I left the building. Expectancy is the key to a quick and bountiful harvest! I know that if God did it for me, He can do it for every sower who is reading these pages and sowing in faith!

Things To Remember From Chapter Three:

1. The picture on the package gives you an idea of what you can reap.

2. You sow according to your appetite.

3. A seed packet will tell you how long it will be before you get a harvest.

4. You can find the right time to sow on the package.

5. Every opportunity has a time limit.

6. Missing an opportunity is the most expensive mistake you will ever make.

7. Your seed has an assignment.

PART II

THE SEED

· · · · · ·

CHAPTER 4

The Millionaire's Seed

**Five secrets told to me by a man who made
ninety-nine million dollars in one year!**

When I was in debt, I was determined not to declare bankruptcy. I would pay every creditor everything I owed them. I did not know how I was going to do this, but God sent a man into my life who helped me develop a three-step plan for financial freedom.

1. *I would bring my finances to even.*
2. *I would take in more money than I spent.*
3. *I would never buy anything that I could not pay for with cash.*

I made the decision that I would not go any further into debt, and with God's help, I would be debt-free. When you read these three steps, it looks like an easy undertaking, but when I planned my strategy, it seemed like an impossibility. But with commitment, determination, and sowing, praise God! Today, I don't owe anyone anything, but to love them.

How did I make these changes in my life? The first thing that had to change was my mentality. My friend told me that I must transform my thinking if I wanted to change my reality.

He taught me the following truths that would revolutionize my thinking:

- *The mind is the ultimate conduit to the spirit.*
- *You must learn to master money or money will master you.*
- *Your thinking affects every decision you make, every prayer you pray, and every seed you sow.*
- *Your situation won't change until your thinking does.*
- *Your faith will never operate above your level of thinking.*

It wasn't until I discovered that *the way I thought about money determined my decisions about money* that I started becoming free. Having been raised in poverty and having lived my entire adult life in debt, I had to change my mind before I could change my financial situation. I had some deep-rooted beliefs about money that I had to overcome.

A good friend gave me a book by Dr. John Avanzini called *Always Abounding.* This book set my heart on fire and made me mad at the devil and myself. I was mad at the devil for lying to me and mad at myself for believing him.

Dr. Avanzini's book, along with the Word of God, began to break the chains of bondage from my mind. After only a few months of reading Dr. Avanzini's books, my entire life turned around. I begin to realize that I could have prosperity in my life.

I want to encourage you with the same thought today: you can have prosperity! It can happen quickly. I am living proof. I was out of debt (without declaring bankruptcy), and I was putting money in the bank within eighteen months. That was thirty-four years ago, and I am still out of debt today. God is helping me live in abundance.

I met Dr. Avanzini in November of 1994 when we were doing a telethon together in California for the TBN Network. He told me that God had spoken to him about my ministry and had shown him that He wanted to use me to change people's financial situations. He said I had gone through what I had gone through because you can never lead people where you have not walked.

Dr. Avanzini laid his hands on me in California and asked God to impart the anointing to break the power of debt from people's lives and to speak the hundred-fold return over their seed. Dr. John Avanzini started me on the study of seedtime and harvest that has resulted in this book. I am eternally grateful for the mentoring he has given to me.

I want you to know that God is enlarging my mind, increasing my revelation of seedenomics, and prospering me supernaturally. I am honored to get to impart this revelation into your life to help you get out or stay out of debt. It all starts in the mind.

We receive numerous letters in our office from people who have given into our ministry, who are now out of debt and are prospering supernaturally. Praise the Lord for His anointing that lifts the burdens and destroys financial yokes from God's people. Poverty mentality is being broken and seedenomics mentality is being birthed. Amen.

Are your money decisions being made from a mindset of debt, lack, want, need, and limited financial resources? If so, your mindset must change. I want to share with you five things that will produce immediate prosperity. I pray that these five things that were told to me in the private jet of a man who made ninety-nine million dollars the year I met him will bring about a change in your life.

. . . .

One: Sow Bigger

. . . .

You will never change the size of your harvest until you change the size of your seed. Financial progress stops at the level of your giving. Many people reach certain levels of giving and never progress any further because they enter comfort zones.

Living in the comfort zone will put you in the poverty zone. When needs are being met, and you have a little extra money left over each month, it is easy to become comfortable.

This is when progress stops, and abundance is forsaken as a goal. When you stop moving forward, you start drifting backward. I've reached certain plateaus in my finances, because of the fear that comes with each step of faith. I hate to admit it, but I've missed bigger harvests by allowing myself to get into what I call a *comfort zone of giving*. I started out giving twenty dollars, then fifty, then a hundred, and then a thousand.

With each level of giving, the harvest increases, but there is a battle each time you start to move up higher. About two weeks ago, I moved to a new level in my giving. It was extremely uncomfortable and fearful. God spoke to me to give a very large gift of several thousand dollars. It was a stretch. I went through a trying time after obeying. I stood strong in faith, and now I am enjoying a time of abundant harvest!

We must not forget that the faith walk is a journey. There may be rest stops, but we must get back on the road to make progress. Faith needs three things to grow bigger, so you can sow bigger, and receive bigger.

- **Your faith must be fed by the Word of God.** You must read Biblical promises concerning finances. Write these promises down and commit them to memory. Speak those promises aloud each day. When negative thoughts come regarding your finances, stand on the Word of God.

- **Your faith must be free from barriers.** If your religion does not believe in or allow for prosperity, then you will not have faith for finances. For most of my life, I had a poverty mentality, and that was blocking God's prosperity. Thoughts that oppose the Word of God must be uprooted and forsaken. Negative or fearful thoughts are roadblocks on the road to abundance. You must remove these barriers.

- **Your faith must be exercised by actions beyond human ability.** In the world of strength, you never know how strong you are until you push yourself to the next level. At each level, you push yourself to get stronger. The same thing is true in the world of faith. I had faith to be saved when I was saved, but I had to exercise that faith by taking action.

I remember when I gave my first large offering of $20. It took faith to give that much at one time. Now I know that doesn't seem like much today, but at the time, it seemed like a thousand. It was all the money I had in the world. If I had never acted on faith, I would never have been able to step out in faith today and give thousands. It all started with the first step of faith—giving that first $20 years ago.

. . . .

Two: Expect Bigger

. . . .

You attract what you expect. God gifted us with the ability to imagine. This frees us to dream. A millionaire has different dreams than the less fortunate. At some point, the millionaire allowed himself to think bigger and expect more. They say once a person accepts their present status, they remain at that status.

Refuse to allow yourself to be locked in the prison of mediocrity. Each thought of impossibility, inability, and unworthiness is a bar in a mental prison. Only you can determine what you expect. Hopeful anticipation is a decision, just as hopelessness is a decision.

> *Mark 11:24 (KJV) Therefore I say to you, What things soever you desire (hope for) when you pray, believe them and you shall have them.*

If you are a mechanic who works for an hourly wage, begin to expect to own your own garage. You may not have a dollar at this moment, but you have faith—and faith can change your financial situation. You also have a God-given creative mind. It's been said that there are no money problems, only idea problems. Money gravitates toward good ideas.

As a songwriter, I know that a song is nothing more than an idea that is put to music. I have written hundreds of songs over the years, and they have resulted in me making thousands of dollars. God was the source of those ideas. He gave me the ability to turn those ideas into money. Each time I receive a check from songwriting royalties, I am reminded that it all began with the first sacrificial gift I gave of $20.

That first act of obedience made it possible for me to give hundreds of thousands of dollars into the work of God over the years.

· · · · · · · · · · · · · ·

Three: Work Harder

· · · · · · · · · · · · · ·

People today are trying everything from the lottery to Las Vegas, trying to get rich enough to quit their job. That mentality always produces failure and defeat. God provides us with an opportunity, but we must take full advantage of the opportunity. We must not confuse activity with accomplishment. Just being busy will make you tired, and it will not get the job done.

To make our work productive, we must remain focused on objectives. To increase focus, answer these questions:

> ➤ *What do you want to accomplish in the next twelve months?*
> ➤ *What do you want to accomplish in the next thirty days?*
> ➤ *What are you going to accomplish today?*

Make a to-do list of seven things you will do each day to improve your life. Success is not exempt from work! I've found that the harder I work, the more opportunity I have for increase and success.

It appears to me today that the socialistic mindset of politicians in the United States is producing a generation who have no work ethic. Every business in our city has help wanted signs posted in their windows, but the unemployment rate is still high. This tells me people don't want to work.

Socialism promises equal wealth, but it only delivers equal poverty. Any time people are dependent on the government instead of God, they are in trouble! God instituted work. The Apostle Paul taught that if a man doesn't work, he doesn't eat. Even Christians today want maximum results with minimum effort. They want to sow a seed and wait for an angel to deliver the money to them. It doesn't work that way.

Your blessing could come in different forms. Your blessing could be the opportunity to work more hours at your company or get promotions for working harder. *Blessings are a by-product of hard work, not a substitute for it*—there is no substitute for hard work. Work is a seed for success and prosperity.

. . . .

Four: Love Bigger

. . . .

For God to bless us as He wants, we need to be baptized in love. Love allows us to use the blessings of God to bless each other.

Love's enemy is greed. It wants to squeeze and hold on to what God has given you. Greed robs, steals, cheats, and abuses. Love adds, gives, helps, and comforts. The one thing that will conquer greed is love.

I love my family, so I give to them and supply their needs. I love God and His work, so I sow into the kingdom so that His work might go forth and prosper. Love will not allow me to sit by when there is a need and not meet that need. I'm a giver who loves to give!

One of the greatest miracles of the Bible happened in Noah's ark. God told Noah to take two of every animal into the ark. Have you ever wondered why the foxes did not eat the chickens, and the cats did not devour the rats? God caused creatures of different natures to live together in harmony because of love.

Love changes our nature. It conquers wrong attitudes, pride, and arrogance. A baptism of love is essential if you desire to live in supernatural abundance. God wants to bless us so we can be a blessing. Love is always giving. Love is the very nature of God. Love cannot be stored; it must flow to grow.

There are only two types of people in the world, givers, and takers. Takers are a reservoir and givers are a river. Which one are you? A reservoir stores water and always remains the same, while the river controls water and grows as it flows. God made everything to give and not just to take in. When a river does not flow, it becomes stagnant and stinky. Nothing can live in this type of water. God's principles will not live and produce in stagnant waters. What damns the river is greed; love breaks through and allows blessings to flow freely.

. . . .

Five: Waste Less

. . . .

This generation seems to be one of abuse and excess. When I was a child growing up in a poor family with nine children, we could never leave the table until we ate all our food. Waste was not permitted in our home, and we were not Christians. Later, I discovered that this was a principle that was practiced by Jesus.

John 6:12 (KJV) Gather up the fragments that remain, that nothing be lost.

Many become careless with the increase. This affects the amount of increase God allows to come into our life. Jesus displays this principle in the parable of the talents in Matthew 25. This parable is about a master who was leaving his house to travel. Before leaving, he entrusted his property to his servants. According to the abilities of each man, one servant received five talents, another received two, and a third received only one.

A talent was a unit of weight of approximately eighty pounds, and when used as a unit of money, was valued for that weight of silver. One talent was worth six thousand denari. A day's wage was one denari. They worked six days every week, therefore one talent was worth around 20 years of wages.

This was a lot of money to be given to servants. So, one servant took his five talents and traded them, and turned them into five more talents. The one who had two talents used his and gained two more talents. But the man who received one talent buried his talent because He was concerned about his master losing money. When the master returned, the ones who had used their talents wisely were praised. The one who had buried his talent had his talent taken away. The master gave his talent to the man who had ten talents.

> *Matthew 25:29 (TLV) For to the one who has, more shall be given, and he shall have an abundance. But from the one who does not have, even what he does have shall be taken away.*

In this parable, Jesus shows us that the man who wasted time and did not invest his talent lost that which he had. He did not use what he had wisely. He wasted what the Master had given Him. If we are time wasters, talent wasters, or money wasters, we must change to have God's greatest blessings. To prosper, we must eliminate fearful thinking, negative thinking, and small thinking.

If you are thinking that everyone cannot be prosperous, then let me ask you: *Why not?* If you believe it cannot happen now, then let me ask you: *When will it happen?* Don't say, "Maybe someday." How about today? How about *right now?*

Just like this millionaire told me: "God's ways are higher than your ways, and His thoughts are higher than your thoughts."

It's time to raise your level of thinking. Think like a sower. Think like a giver. Develop a millionaire mindset. Millionaires expect a big harvest, so they sow bigger seeds resulting in a bigger blessing. Don't waste your time on small thinking. Think BIG. Say, "Lord, bless me to be a blessing!"

Things To Remember From Chapter Four:

1. *Either you learn to master money or money will master you.*

2. *Unless your mentality changes, your money will never change.*

3. *You will never change the size of your harvest until you change the size of your seed.*

4. *Living in the comfort zone will put you in the poverty zone.*

5. *You attract what you expect.*

6. *Blessings are a by-product of hard work, not a substitute for it.*

7. *Waste less and think bigger.*

CHAPTER 5

The Solomon Seed

The Seed of 1000!

2 Chronicles 1:6–12 (NKJV) *Solomon went up there to the bronze altar before the Lord, which was at the tabernacle of meeting, and offered a thousand burnt offerings on it. On that night God appeared to Solomon, and said to him, "Ask what shall I give you?"*

"And Solomon said to God: '' You have shown great mercy to David, my father, and have made me king in his place. "Now, O Lord God, let your promise to David my father be established, for you have made me king over a people like the dust of the earth in multitude. "Now give me wisdom and knowledge, that I may go out and come in before this people; for who can judge this great people of yours?"

Then God said to Solomon: "Because this was in your heart and you have not asked riches or wealth or honor or the life of your enemies, nor have you asked long life, but asked wisdom and knowledge for yourself, that

*you may judge my people over whom I have made you
king "wisdom and knowledge are granted to you, and
I will give you; and I will give you riches and wealth
and honor, such as none of the kings have had who
were before you, nor shall any after you have the like."*

It was customary in Solomon's culture to offer one sacrifice. Solomon did not do what culture demanded—he gave one thousand sacrifices. As I was reading this story, I began to wonder what inspired Solomon to offer one thousand sacrifices. This motivated me to investigate this number *one thousand*. I knew there had to be a reason Solomon went beyond cultural protocol. In studying, I discovered that God counts by thousands. Over five hundred and twenty-one times in scripture, *one thousand* is used.

The Hebrew alphabet has only letters. The letters also represent numbers. The first letter which would be our A is *Alef*. When used at the beginning of the Hebrew years, it means one thousand. It is just difficult for me to believe that this is a coincidence. This is yet another reason I believe this number is significant to God and should be to us!

Look at these references in scripture to the number one thousand **(emphasis added)**:

- *Deuteronomy 1:11 (KJV) The Lord God of your fathers make you a **thousand** times so many more as ye are, and bless you, as he hath promised you!*
- *Joshua 23:10 (AMPC) One man of you shall put to flight a **thousand**...*
- *Judges 15:16 (KJV) And Samson said, With the jawbone of an ass, heaps upon heaps, with the jaw of an ass have I slain a **thousand** men.*
- *Psalm 105:8 (MSG) And he remembers, remembers his Covenant—for a **thousand** generations he's been as good as his word.*

- *Song Of Solomon 8:11 (KJV) Solomon had a vineyard at Baal-hamon; He let out the vineyard unto keepers; Every one for the fruit thereof was to bring a **thousand** pieces of silver.*
- *Psalm 50:10 (KJV) For every beast of the forest is mine, and the cattle upon a **thousand** hills.*
- *Ezra 2: (KJV) Also Cyrus the king brought forth the vessels of the house of the Lord, which Nebuchadnezzar had brought forth out of Jerusalem, and had put them in the house of his gods; Even those did Cyrus king of Persia bring forth by the hand of Mithredath the treasurer, and numbered them unto Sheshbazzar, the prince of Judah. And this is the number of them: thirty chargers of gold, a **thousand** chargers of silver, nine and twenty knives, Thirty basons of gold, silver basons of a second sort four hundred and ten, and other vessels a **thousand.***
- *2 Peter 3:8 (NKJV) But, beloved, do not forget this one thing, that with the Lord one day is as a **thousand** years, and a **thousand** years as one day.*
- *Revelation 20:6 (KJV) But the rest of the dead lived not again until the **thousand** years were finished. This is the first resurrection. Blessed and holy is he that hath part in the first resurrection: on such the second death hath no power, but they shall be priests of God and of Christ, and shall reign with him a **thousand** years. And when the **thousand** years are expired, Satan shall be loosed out of his prison…*

There's an interesting story about one thousand in Genesis 20:16–18. Abraham lied to King Abimelech and told him Sarah was his sister and not his wife. This caused the King to take Sarah into his house to make her part of his harem. When he did this, his house was cursed. Every female was barren. No children were being born. The King realized what had happened, so he returned Sarah to Abraham and brought one thousand pieces of silver. When he did this, God lifted the curse from his house and the maidservants began to bear children again.

I also believe by divine order of God the number one thousand appears in other places to confirm that this number is special to God. When Solomon offered one thousand sacrifices, it moved the hand of God and brought Solomon the favor of God.

Some would disagree with me, saying that the number one thousand is not significant. They say it's just like any other number. While I respect their conclusion, I must differ with them. There are too many references and testimonies about seeds of one thousand for me not to be totally convinced it is a number that causes God to respond. Consider this:

$$1000=10^3 \text{ One thousand is ten to the third power}$$
$$(10 \times 1=10, 10 \times 10=100, 10 \times 100=1000)$$

Ten is a number used quite frequently by God:

- Genesis 10:10—first verse that mentions the kingdom.
- Man was created with ten fingers and ten toes.
- Abraham was the 10th descendant of Adam.
- There were ten plagues in Egypt.
- God gave Ten Commandments.
- The tithe is 10%.

. . . .

Solomon's Sacrifice

. . . .

God said because of Solomon's one thousand sacrifices, He would give him five things:

➢ *Wisdom*
➢ *Knowledge*
➢ *Riches*
➢ *Wealth*
➢ *Honor*

God said He would have these attributes like no other king before him or after him. There was a prophetic word from God spoken over his seed of one thousand offerings. Did it come to pass? Let's look at the evidence from the Word of God:

1. **Wisdom:** The Bible tells us that Solomon was wiser than all men, and he was famous for his wisdom in all the nations round about.

    1 Kings 4:29-31 (KJV) *And God gave Solomon wisdom and understanding exceeding much, and largeness of heart, even as the sand that is on the sea shore. And Solomon's wisdom excelled the wisdom of all the children of the east country, and all the wisdom of Egypt. For he was wiser than all men; than Ethan the Ezrahite, and Heman, and Chalcol, and Darda, the sons of Mahol: and his fame was in all nations round about.*

2. **Knowledge:** Solomon's knowledge was so extensive that people came from far and near to hear him speak.

    1 Kings 4:32-34 (KJV) *And he spake three thousand proverbs: and his songs were a thousand and five.*
    And he spake of trees, from the cedar tree that is in Lebanon even unto the hyssop that springeth out of the wall: he spake also of beasts, and of fowl, and of creeping things, and of fishes. And there came of all people to hear the wisdom of Solomon, from all kings of the earth, which had heard of his wisdom.

3. **Riches:** The riches of Solomon were greater than the riches of any other king.

    1 Kings 10:23 (KJV) *So Solomon exceeded all the kings of the earth for riches and for wisdom.*

4. **Wealth:** 1 Kings 10:21; 27 (KJV) Solomon had so much gold, his drinking glasses were made of gold. He had so much silver, that it wasn't even counted in his total wealth.

    And all king Solomon's drinking vessels were of gold, and all the vessels of the house of the forest of Lebanon were of pure gold; none were of silver: it was nothing accounted of in the days of Solomon...
    And the king made silver to be in Jerusalem as stones, and cedars made he to be as the sycomore trees that are in the vale, for abundance.

5. **Honor:** Solomon was held in such honor and esteem that many came yearly from everywhere to hear him and bring him gifts.

    1 Kings 10:24-25 (KJV) *And all the earth sought to Solomon, to hear his wisdom, which God had put in his heart.*
    And they brought every man his present, vessels of silver, and vessels of gold, and garments, and armour, and spices, horses, and mules, a rate year by year.

    Our seeds define us!
    Our seeds predict our future!
    Our seeds release our destiny!
    Our seeds get God's attention!
    Our seeds garner God's affection!
    Our seeds birth a season of favor!
    Our seeds create an attraction for blessings!

God orchestrates our deliverance, but our seeds initiate our release from bondage!

. . . .

Ten Things Happen When You
Plant A $1,000 Seed

. . . .

1. Your Seed Activates Increase!

Whether we sow corn, tomatoes, or money, that seed will multiply! That seed releases God's promise made through Paul the Apostle: *God gives seed to the sower and multiplies the seed that is sown (2 Corinthians 9:10 KJV).* Sowing a seed will do what prayer, praise, and righteous living alone cannot do! Seed is the only element in creation to which God attached a harvest.

2. Your Seed Sets Increase Into Motion!

Your seed schedules a harvest in your life. Hosea the Prophet declares:

> Hosea 6:11 (NKJV) *Also, O Judah, a harvest is appointed for you, When I return the captives of My people.*

The Bible tells us there is a time to sow and a time to reap. The Bible also declares there is a due season on every seed that is sown. Once you release seed in the natural, your due season is released in the spiritual.

> Ecclesiastes 3:2 (TLB) *A time to be born; A time to die; A time to plant; A time to harvest;*

3. Your Seed Lifts Up A Standard Against Poverty, Lack, And Shortage!

Your seed launches an offensive attack against the devil who comes to steal, kill, and destroy. Your seed stops him in his tracks, intercepts his intentions, spoils his plans, and reverses his decisions concerning you!

> Malachi 3:11 (KJV) *Neither shall your vine cast her fruit before the time in the field.*

Business deals, property sales, investments, and all financial transactions will not be aborted or unsuccessful. Your seed will speak for you!

4. Your Seed Declares That You Are A Sower!

God will bless a sower. Genesis 26 shows us Isaac sowing in famine. There had been no rain, and people were starving to death. Instead of keeping his seed and eating it, Isaac sowed it.

God was so impressed with Isaac's faith that He sent rain and gave Isaac a hundred-fold increase! God recognizes sowers because He said He is the one who gives seed to sowers.

5. Your Seed Defies Greed!

A man who holds on to what he has opens the door to poverty.

> Proverbs 11:24–26 (KJV) *There is that scattereth, and yet increaseth; and there is that withholdeth more than is meet, but it tendeth to poverty.*
>
> *The liberal soul shall be made fat: and he that watereth shall be watered also himself.*
>
> *He that withholdeth corn, the people shall curse him: but blessing shall be upon the head of him that selleth it.*

The one who sows will increase. People shall curse the one who holds onto his seed and refuses to sow it. Greed can destroy a family, a church, and a country. In our beloved country of America, I see so much greed! God so loved that He gave. If we are going to be like God, we must be sowers.

6. Your Seed Confirms Faith!

Money is the one tangible thing we can attach our faith to as we sow. Money represents us—our work, our talent, and our income! God is honored when we release something personal to receive something precious.

In 2 Kings 4, a rich woman gave the prophet a bed to sleep in. She gave it in faith so that she could receive what she desired in return—a child. To hold on to what we have is an act of fear; to release what we have is an act of faith!

7. Your Seed Gets God's Attention!

Acts 10 talks about Cornelius. When God saw his sowing and heard his praying, He began to set things in motion to answer Cornelius' prayer. He employed one of His preachers named Peter who was praying on a rooftop in Joppa.

Cornelius was not on God's list of people to bless. He was a Gentile, and his culture was not part of God's plan. He changed God's agenda when he sowed.

Cornelius had many people at his house, and they all received the baptism of the Holy Spirit because of Cornelius' sowing and prayers.

8. Your Seed Moves God's Hand!

> Luke 6:38 (KJV) *Give, and it shall be given unto you; good measure, pressed down, and shaken together, and running over, shall men give into your bosom. For with the same measure that ye mete withal it shall be measured to you again.*

A doctor's testimony: A doctor walked by me one Sunday morning after I preached and handed me a check for $1,000. He said, "I need a miracle. My practice is going under, and I have a mountain of debt." I took his hand, and we prayed over his seed. I asked God to turn things around for this physician.

I was back in that area about fifteen months later and this man came up to me and told me his story. He said, "Two weeks after I gave you that check for your ministry, I received a call from another prominent doctor who wanted to have lunch with me. We merged our practices, and we just opened our third clinic!"

God brought these two men together for a miracle! I have seen this man several times since that then and he always tells me, "The greatest decision I've ever made was sowing that $1,000 seed into your ministry!"

My wife's testimony: *My* wife, Lori, is alive today because of a $1,000 seed. She was in intensive care for seven days, and doctors could not help her. On the seventh day, I heard the Holy Spirit tell me that everything would be okay.

My pastor was coming to visit that afternoon. As I waited on him, I felt strongly impressed to sow a $1,000 seed into my pastor's life. I would give that seed an instruction.

So, when he arrived, I handed him the seed. I said, "Pastor, this is my act of obedience to God's voice for my wife's healing." He prayed a simple prayer and left. I had been at the hospital for seven days. After my pastor left, I felt led to kiss my wife goodbye and go get a good night's rest.

On the way home, I knew I would not sleep, but I did! In fact, I slept until six a.m. I got up quickly, showered and dressed, and was back at the hospital by seven a.m.

My wife had not eaten in seven days. When I arrived that eighth morning, she was up, with her make-up on and her hair fixed. When she saw me, she said, "I am starving to death!"

She told me a man whom she assumed was a doctor came into

the intensive care unit earlier that morning, sat on her bed, and told her things would be all right. The nurse said that no one but my wife had been in that room. I believe God sent an angel! It's been almost five years, and my wife has never had another problem.

They say a man with an argument is at the mercy of a man with experience. I am a living witness—as many of you are—that when God moves us to sow, He moves others, even angels, to deliver our harvest.

9. Your Seed Proves The Devil Is A Liar!

When God speaks to us to sow, Satan is always there to tell us every reason why we can't.

- *If you keep the seed God is telling you to sow, then you have proven Satan is right about you.*
- *When you sow that seed, it proves Satan is a liar concerning you and your seed.*
- *When you get the harvest from your seed, it proves the devil is a liar again.*

The devil says, "You can't trust God. If you sow that seed, you will never get it back. You are insane for giving your money away." He is silent when the harvest comes. Don't believe the lie—stick with the proof. The devil is a liar!

10. Your Seed Accelerates Prosperity!

> Proverbs 13:22 (KJV) *A good man leaveth an inheritance to his children's children: and the wealth of the sinner is laid up for the just.*

That wealth will eventually find its way into the hands of the righteous. God is looking for people to bless and prosper. He gets pleasure when His children live in abundance.

It's said that ten men control fifty percent of the world's wealth. In these last days, that wealth—and other new wealth—is going to begin to find its way into the hands of believers to help finance the end-time move of God on the earth.

Are you a candidate for wealth transfer? Here is what the Lord said to me, *"If you finance the end-time harvest, you will harvest the end-time finance."*

During the first year of this man-made pandemic, COVID-19, it has been reported that eleven trillion dollars of new wealth was released on the earth. Many more trillions will be released soon. Your seed will position you for the end-time finance God is releasing!

. . . .

Thousand Dollar Seed

. . . .

There is an envelope laying on my desk that I am looking at as I write these words. It came to me years ago in a meeting up on the east coast. I have carried it with me since the first night I received it.

I was preaching in a church there, and I was raising money for a missionary trip I was taking to Central America. I was asking the ones who could if they would sow a $1,000 seed! I told them you can't go, but you can send me. I can't go without your financial support. I asked for ten people who could help me. I had ten envelopes in my hand, and nine people responded.

As I stood there, a very sweet lady walked up and said, "I would love to do that, but I don't have it."

I said, "Take the envelope and fill out the card on the inside. When you get it, you can send it."

After service, she walked up and handed me the envelope and the card. Taped to the card was all the money she had, which was four quarters. She told me a very heartbreaking story.

Her husband of twenty-four years had left her and her teenage daughter and divorced her. She had no job, no money, and was about to lose her home. Her daughter had hitchhiked to New Orleans and become a call girl. She was sending her mom a little money to live on. The woman told me, "I know my daughter is called to the ministry. Would you pray for her return to God? And please pray for me to get a job. So, I prayed!

A few weeks later, I received a letter from this lady and a check for one hundred dollars. She wrote, "I got a job with a man in our church who has a cleaning company. We pray every morning before work. He has thirty-five employees and fifteen trucks, and we clean commercial buildings. I love my job."

Each month, I would get a check for one hundred dollars. She would always ask me to pray for her daughter. I laid her letter, like I do all letters, on my altar in my office, and I prayed.

On the third month, she sent her check and said, "I was at church on Wednesday night, and my daughter came down the aisle, fell at the altar, and repented. She had hitch-hiked with a truck driver back to her home church.

She said she had been standing on a street corner, selling her body, when a large man walked up and said, "Your mother has been praying and sowing seeds for you. Now, go home and get your life right because God has a purpose for you."

This has been a few years ago. That girl went to Bible college, and she now operates a halfway house for runaways and those dealing with drug issues.

Eleven months after I got the first check from this lady, her boss told her he was selling the company. She tried to get a loan to buy it but was turned down by every lending institution. One Sunday morning, this man and his wife walked up to her at church. They handed her a set of keys, and they told her God had spoken to them to give her the company. The company was debt-free, and they had a million dollars' worth of contracts with various companies that would last for many years.

God brought this lady from having four quarters taped to a card to a million-dollar debt-free business—and a daughter who had been saved and delivered—in less than a year. *This is the power of the right seed, at the right place, at the right time.*

There is no doubt in my mind that a $1,000 seed will generate an influx of blessing into your life. Something supernatural happens when you cross that threshold in your giving. For many people, though, giving a $1,000 seed requires a greater level of faith than they are accustomed to exercising.

I encourage you to meditate on the scriptures and testimonies in this chapter. Your faith will grow, and your ability to hear God will grow. Because of that, when God speaks to you to elevate your giving to the $1,000 level, you will be ready!

Things To Remember From Chapter Five:

1. *God counts by thousands.*

2. *Your seed activates increase. God blesses a sower.*

3. *Your seed breaks the back of lack, poverty, and shortage.*

4. *Your seed will defy greed.*

5. *Money is one tangible thing to which we can attach our faith.*

6. *Your seed gets God's attention and moves His hand.*

7. *Your seed proves the devil is a liar and accelerates prosperity.*

CHAPTER 6

The Third-Day Generation Seed

The Power Of The Third Day

In the Garden of Eden, God told Satan that He would put enmity between Satan and the woman, and between his seed and her seed. God said, "Her seed shall bruise your head, and you will bruise her seed's heel." This is the introduction of the Third-Day generation seed.

Man watches as God tells Satan. "I am giving her seed the power to defeat you. I am giving her seed the power to put you under His feet. You will never be able to rule over her seed."

I want you to know that no matter how hard the enemy tries, we have been given victory over him. Jesus rose on the Third Day, making Him the ultimate Third-Day seed. As He is in this world, so are we. God gave you and me the power as the Third-Day seed generation to overcome every situation that we face with Satan.

In His Word, God shows us the importance of being the Third-Day generation seed. God uses the number *three* to tell the story of redemption throughout the scriptures.

- Four hundred sixty-seven times, the number *three* appears in the text.
- We see *three* men mentioned by God as early as before the flood that destroyed the earth—Abel, Enoch, and Noah.
- Noah had *three* sons: Shem, Ham, and Japheth.
- We also see the power of *three* in the promise of God to the generations of Abraham: First, to Abraham, then to his son, Isaac, then to his son, Jacob.

Not only is the number *three* important, but we also see the mention of the *Third* Day. On the Third Day, prophets like Jonah are dropped off at seaside ports by a giant fish. The Third Day is the day that stone gods like Dagon come tumbling down, and God starts coming home to His people. The Third Day is the day when prisoners of Pharaoh were set free.

The Third Day is the day the people come to the mountains and the mountains shake and the rivers are parted. The Third Day is the day when people enter the Promised Land. The Third Day is the day when Harem girls like Esther face down powerful giant kings. The Third Day is the day stones are rolled away. The Third Day is the day a crucified carpenter came back to life. This is the power of the Third Day generation!

. . . .

Third-Day Promises: Potential

. . . .

On the Third Day, many things are released from the hand of God. There is **potential** released on the Third Day. God created the seed on the Third Day. In the seed, He placed potential. He placed in every seed the potential to bring forth a harvest.

. . . .

Third-Day Promises: Provision

. . . .

There is a **provision** released in the Third Day. I want to illustrate this provision by looking at Abraham.

When Abraham was seventy-five years old, God spoke to him and said He would give him a son, and that son would birth a nation. God promised to give Abraham a seed.

> *Genesis 13:14-16 (KJV) Lift up now thine eyes.... For all the land which thou seest, to thee will I give it, and to thy seed forever. And I will make thy seed as the dust of the earth.*

> *Romans 4:17–21 (KJV) As it is written I have made thee a father of many nations, before him whom he believed, even God who quickeneth the dead, and calleth those things that be not as they were. Who against hope believed in hope that he might become the father of many nations.*

> *According to that which was spoken, So shall thy seed be. And being not weak in faith, considered not his own body now dead when he was about a hundred years old, neither the deadness of Sara's womb: He staggered not at the promise of God through unbelief: but was strong in faith giving glory to God. And being fully persuaded that, what God had promised, he was able to perform.*

This is monumental because this is where we see an example of God giving seed to the sower. Abraham was given a promise, but God provided the seed. Abraham went to bed with no seed to sow. His body, ninety-nine years old, had ceased to produce seed.

Abraham was now almost one hundred years old. It had been almost twenty-five years since the promise had been given to Abraham—and still no seed. But somewhere in the middle of the night, Abraham had seed and the ability to sow that seed.

The seed that was given to Abraham was the nation of Israel. Twenty-five years later, this prophecy came to pass. God does not get in a hurry! God had to wait until it took a miracle for this to take place. Yet today, we are still witnessing the magnitude of Abraham's seed.

Twenty-five years after God promised a child, we hear this sound: "Waah, waah!" That is the cry of Abraham's son coming from the tent. Sarah has just given birth at ninety years of age. Abraham just had Willard Scott read his name on the Today show and wish him a happy one-hundredth birthday. The Enquirer has Abraham and Sarah on the front page. Fox News stops talking about politics long enough to announce this miraculous birth: a one-hundred-year-old man and a ninety-year-old woman have a baby. They name him Isaac, which means *laughter*. Don't tell me God doesn't have a sense of humor!

When it looked impossible in the natural, God let the world know that He is still able to make something out of what looks like nothing.

I want to encourage you *today. When God speaks to you, hold on to the promise of God. It will come to pass. God will provide the seed when He gives you a promise.*

The miracle was that Abraham had been given seed, and the promise had come to pass. However, once the promise came to pass in Abraham's life, we see something that is surprising. Have you ever had God surprise you after you received a promise? Has God ever spoken to you to put the promise that you have waited for so long on the altar?

This is where we find Abraham. After God gave Abraham this son, He asked for the son back. God spoke to Abraham and told him to take the son and offer him for a sacrifice. He said, "Abraham, take your seed and build an altar to me for the sacrifice of your seed."

Genesis 22:4 (KJV) Then on the third day Abraham lifted up his eyes, and saw the place afar off.

Notice what the text says: "*on the third day.*" It was not a coincidence that Abraham would offer Isaac on the Third Day. Abraham was commanded to sow a Third-Day Seed. God was asking Abraham if he was willing to return and sow what had been given to him. God wanted to show Abraham on that day that He was Jehovah Jireh or *the Lord that provides.*

Abraham did as the Lord commanded. Abraham was obedient to the voice of the Lord even when it looked like the harvest from his seed was about to be killed. Abraham laid Isaac upon the altar. Just as Abraham was about to sacrifice Isaac, an angel's hand grabbed his hand and stopped him from taking the life of his son.

It was then that God showed him a ram to put on the altar. The ram was a type of Jesus being offered for the sins of man as God's seed for man's deliverance. This story lets us know that God provides seeds to the sower and a plan of redemption to every believer. God gave His son Jesus as a seed to give us eternal life. There is redemption in the Third-Day seed sown by a Third-Day man.

. . . .

Third-Day Promises: Power

. . . .

There is **power** on the Third Day. In the book of *Hosea*, there is a message that brings power to the hearer:

Hosea 6:1–3 (KJV) Come, let us return to the Lord; For He has torn, but He will heal us; He has stricken, but He will bind us up. After two days He will revive us; On the third day He will raise us up, that we may live in His sight. Let us know, let us pursue the

knowledge of the Lord. He will come to us like rain,
Like the latter and former rain to the earth.

This is talking about a time when the Holy Spirit comes to put new life in His people. The Holy Spirit comes to bring us a spiritual lift. He comes to prepare us for new dimensions in Himself. These new dimensions are accompanied by new warfare or confrontation. *Each new level comes with a new devil.*

The Bible tells us that after two days, He will revive us. The word *revive* here means to bring back to life. It is a revisiting of a place or time where we have once been. The Bible then tells us that after the Third Day, He will raise us up!

To be raised up means to be equipped with everything we need to go to a place where we have never been. He wants to take us somewhere in our sowing that we have never been before. He is not sending us empty-handed. He is sending us with renewed purity, power, and authority. He is raising us up on the Third Day to go to a new level in Him. He is raising up a Third-Day generation.

God wants to raise up a kingdom of believers as an army of power and authority to cast out devils, heal the sick, and reap the harvest. He is looking for individuals who will stand up for what is right and proclaim that God is a God of miracles, a God of the supernatural, and a God of prosperity.

He is raising up a Third-Day generation who will both practice and live *seedtime and harvest.* He is looking for individuals who will step out of their comfort zone and sow faith seeds. He desires people who will listen to the voice of the Holy Spirit and attack debt head-on. He is seeking those who will *sow where they want to go and want to grow.*

He says that for those who will arise and plant, He will cause the rain to fall and water the seed. He is saying, "You do the sowing; I'll do the watering."

In Hosea 6, He tells us that He will come to us like the latter and former rain. The latter rain falls in September and October.

The latter rain is the rain that washes away the remnants of last year's harvest. It washes away the wheat from the tares, allowing the ground to be prepared for planting. The former rain falls in March and April. This is the rain that waters the seeds that have been planted and ignites them for a harvest.

What God is telling us through the prophet Hosea is that we need to be part of the Third-Day generation—the ones who will return to the Lord and follow His commands and principles and be revived, restored, and blessed. God is calling sowers who will arise and proclaim their place in the kingdom. He is raising up a Third-Day generation who will see a harvest quickly from the seeds that they sow. He is looking for a Third-Day generation who will sow a Third-Day seed. He wants to release power in the life of the sower.

. . . .

Third-Day Promises: Presence

. . . .

There is **presence** in the Third Day. Moses was a Third-Day man leading a Third-Day people. After God's people had been in Egyptian bondage for four hundred and thirty years, God sent Moses to deliver them. Their deliverance would be a picture of what Jesus would accomplish for humanity.

Moses was present with the Israelites, God's people, interceding for their deliverance. We see that after the ten plagues came upon the Egyptians, Pharaoh offered Moses three compromises when the Israelites were ready to leave Egypt. Moses, after being instructed by God, told Pharaoh, "Let my people go!" We see in the following scripture the answers Moses received from Pharaoh:

> *Exodus 8:25–27 (MSG) Pharaoh called in Moses and Aaron and said, "Go ahead. Sacrifice to your God— but do it here in this country."*

Exodus 8:28 (MSG) Pharaoh said, "All right. I'll release you to go and sacrifice to your GOD in the wilderness. Only don't go too far . . ."

Exodus 10:24 (MSG) Pharaoh called in Moses: "Go and worship God. Leave your flocks and herds behind . . ."

Moses, as a part of the Third-Day generation, would not compromise but instead stood his ground. When you are a part of the Third-Day generation, you don't compromise. Each time, Moses responded to Pharaoh by saying, "We will go a full three-day's journey."

He was present with them as they left Egypt. Three days would take them to the Red Sea. They would leave Egypt on the fourteenth day of the month and cross the Red Sea on the seventeenth day—a three-day's journey.

Their journey would be a type and shadow of the death, burial, and resurrection of Jesus. Also, it would be a type of man's deliverance, salvation, baptism in water, and being baptized in the Holy Spirit. It is a type and shadow of your deliverance as well. God is present with you as you walk as part of the Third-Day generation.

. . . .

Third-Day Promises: Types and Shadows

. . . .

We see **types and shadows** of the Third-Day generation throughout the children of Israel's journey:

1. *The Ark of the Covenant contained three things: a jar of manna, Aaron's rod, and the tables of stones (Ten Commandments).*
2. *Moses implemented three types of sacrifices: Sin-offering, peace offering, and praise offering.*

3. *Three laws ruled Israel's conduct: moral, ceremonial, and civil.*
4. *Prayers were offered three times a day.*
5. *Three feasts were established and at the appointed time of the feasts, they brought an offering.*

No one could appear before the Lord without a Third-Day offering. Also, we read during this journey:

> *Exodus 19:10–11 (NKJV) Then the Lord said to Moses, "Go to the people and consecrate them today and tomorrow and let them wash their clothes. And let them be ready for the third day. for on the third day the Lord will come down upon Mount Sinai in the sight of all the people.*

> Exodus 19:16–18 (NKJV) *Then it came to pass on the third day, in the morning, that there were thunderings and lightnings, and a thick cloud on the mountain; and the sound of the trumpet was very loud, so that all the people who were in the camp trembled.*

> *And Moses brought the people out of the camp to meet with God, and they stood at the foot of the mountain. Now Mount Sinai was completely in smoke, because the LORD descended upon it in fire. Its smoke ascended like the smoke of a furnace, and the whole mountain quaked greatly.*

Moses, a part of the Third-Day generation, was leading God's people through the wilderness. Moses, a Third-Day man, led God's people within three days of the Promised Land. After the shortest obituary in history—

> *Joshua 1:2 (NKJV) Moses, my servant is dead.*

—a new Third-Day man named Joshua took over.

So now, Joshua is at the edge of entering the Promised Land. What should have been a fourteen-day journey has lasted for forty years. Unbelief, fear, and disobedience had delayed them forty years. So now they stand ready to enter the Promised Land. After forty years, Joshua and Israel are going to have A Third-Day experience. Look at the instructions that Joshua gave the people:

> *Joshua 1:10–11 (NKJV) Then Joshua com-manded the officers of the people, saying, "Pass through the camp and command the people, saying, 'Prepare provisions for yourselves, for within three days you will cross over this Jordan, to go in to possess the land which the Lord your God is giving you to possess.*

Joshua and Israel entered their Promised Land on the Third Day! That is what happens when the Third-Day generation is obedient to the Word of the Lord.

Third-Day Promises: Healing

There is also ***healing*** that is released on the Third Day. Look what happened to Hezekiah when He prayed on the Third Day:

> *2 Kings 20:4–5 (NKJV) And it happened before Isaiah had gone out into the middle court, that the word of the Lord came to him, saying, "Return and tell Hezekiah the leader of My people, 'Thus says the Lord, the God of David your father: "I have heard your prayer, I have seen your tears; surely I will heal you. On the third day, you shall go up to the house of the Lord.*

Isaiah had told him to put his house in order because he was going to die. When Hezekiah repented, God changed His mind. God added years to his life. The prayers of a Third-Day person can move God's hand and change God's mind about how to bless you.

. . . .

Third-Day Promises: Favor

. . . .

There is *favor* released on the Third Day. Esther was part of a harem, but look what happened!

> *Esther 5:1–2 (NKJV) Now it happened on the third day that Esther put on her royal robes and stood in the inner court of the king's palace, across from the king's house, while the king sat on his royal throne in the royal house, facing the entrance of the house.*
>
> *So it was when the king saw Queen Esther standing in the court, that she found favor in his sight, and the king held out to Esther the golden scepter that was in his hand. Then Esther went near and touched the top of the scepter.*

This Third-Day woman got the King's attention and won the King's favor. When you understand that you are a part of the Third-Day generation, your Third Day brings favor into your life. A Third-Day person walks in favor, sows in favor, and lives in favor.

. . . .

Third-Day Promises: Harvest of Blessings

. . . .

There is a *harvest of blessings* in the Third Day. Second Chronicles 20 says it took three days to gather the spoils of battle!

As Jehoshaphat and his armies faced their enemies and defeated them, it took three days to gather their spoils of battle! When you are a part of the Third-Day generation, you are part of the Third-Day harvest of blessings.

Not only will God send armies against your enemies and make them turn and annihilate themselves, but He will also bless you so much in the process that it will take you three days to carry away your blessing. God is the God of overflow blessings for the Third-Day generation.

. . . .

Third-Day Promises: Restoration

. . . .

There is **restoration** released on the Third Day. In 1 Samuel 30, we read the story of David at Ziklag. Ziklag was invaded, David's family was captured, and everything he owned was stolen. But David was standing in the enemy's camp three days later, reunited with his family and gathering all the spoils the enemy had taken from him.

David had been standing in the ashes of Ziklag when God spoke to Him that he would recover all. David made up his mind that he was not going to bury his destiny in the ashes of his adversity. This lets you know it's not what you have lost that matters, but what you have left.

You must stop *eulogizing the seed* that you may have lost and *start utilizing the seed* you have left. David used what he had and overtook and recovered everything. What David did not know at the time was that Saul would be dead in three days and that he himself would be anointed king.

There is something supernatural that God does for the Third-Day sowers. David was faithful in doing what God called him to do. Three days later, the enemy who was trying to kill him ended up being eliminated.

When you are part of the Third-Day generation, and you sow Third-Day seeds, God will take care of your enemies. It may look impossible, but God will turn it around for your good.

· · · · · · · · · · · · ·

Third-Day Promises: Miracles

· · · · · · · · · · · · ·

There are **miracles** released on the Third Day. Let's look at the ministry of Jesus. Jesus was of the Third-Day generation. His first miracle took place on the Third Day!

> *John 2:1–5 (NKJV) On the third day, there was a wedding in Cana of Galilee, and the mother of Jesus was there. Now both Jesus and His disciples were invited to the wedding. And when they ran out of wine, the mother of Jesus said to Him, "They have no wine." Jesus said to her, "Woman, what does your concern have to do with Me? My hour has not yet come." His mother said to the servants, "Whatever He says to you, do it."*

Jesus performed His first miracle of multiplication on the Third Day. There is something about a Third-Day seed that unlocks a supernatural harvest. I think it is because Jesus was the Third-Day seed that would pay the debt man owed to God.

· · · · · · · · · · · · ·

Third-Day Promises: Salvation

· · · · · · · · · · · · ·

The last thing that is released on the Third Day is **salvation**.

> *John 19:41–42 (NKJV) And in the garden a new tomb in which no one had yet been laid. So there they laid Jesus…*

Here we see the seed of God being sown in a garden. In a garden, there are two types of seeds that can be sown. There are annual seeds and perennial seeds. Annual seeds are sown each new season. Perennial seeds are only sown one time.

Grass is a perennial; it comes back year after year. It can push its way up through concrete or stone. Jesus was a perennial seed. The stone could not hold Him in the grave—a perennial seed can move stones.

The King set a watch over the grave. Ribbons were placed across the stone and held in place with a substance that contained the Kings' seal, to ensure that the body would not be stolen. Hell assigned demons to make sure Jesus remained in the tomb.

I can see it now. The first morning, Satan asks, "How things are going?"

"He's still here," they say. The second day, he received the same response. But on the Third Day (the day seed was created), angels came and rolled back the stone. All could see that the grave was empty—and it still is to this day.

While hell was having a party, Jesus walked down the corridors of the doomed and the damned and interrupted the celebration. He grabbed the keys to death, hell, and the grave. He unlocked the gates of Paradise where saints from the age's past were being held because the way into the presence of God had not yet been prepared. He ascended, and the spirits of those who had died before Calvary went with him. They stopped in Jerusalem and were seen by many.

The seed of God had become the first fruits, not of resurrection, but re-creation. Others like Lazarus had resurrected, but no one had been re-created. Because of what Jesus did, we are born again as re-created beings. We will not die; we will have eternal life.

Now when a person dies in the Lord, they go into the presence of God. We are all seeds of God, and one day, our bodies will be resurrected, and we will be glorified. We will rule and reign on this earth with Christ. That's the awesome power of a seed!

Every time you sow a financial seed into the kingdom of God, your seed is a celebration of the seed God sowed for your salvation.

It is no mystery why hell hates sowers. It is also no mystery why God loves sowers and moves for them as they sow.

Are you part of the Third-Day generation of givers? Does God have access to what is in your hand? If He spoke to you right now to sow everything you have, would you obey? God only trusts you with what you are willing to release. For Him to give you more, you must be willing to hear His voice and obey Him. Don't miss your opportunity to become part of the Third-Day generation. All it takes is acting in obedience.

Things To Remember From Chapter Six:

1. No matter how hard the devil tries, he is still under your feet.

2. Every seed has a potential harvest.

3. God gives seed to the sower. He will provide seed when He gives you a promise.

4. Be faithful even if God asks for your harvest.

5. When we return to the principles, God will revive and raise us up.

6. When you are a part of the Third-Day generation, you don't compromise.

7. You must stop eulogizing the seed that you may have lost and start utilizing the seed you have left.

PART III

WEEDENOMICS

· · · · · ·

CHAPTER 7

Weedenomics Vs. Seedenomics

Jesus spoke twenty-seven parables to His disciples on the financial foundation of the kingdom of God, Seedenomics. In this parable, He deals with the other side of the issue—weedenomics!

> *Matthew 13:18–23 (MSG) Study this story of the farmer planting seed. When anyone hears news of the kingdom and doesn't take it in, it just remains on the surface, and so the Evil One comes along and plucks it right out of that person's heart. This is the seed the farmer scatters on the road.*
>
> *The seed cast in the gravel—this is the person who hears and instantly responds with enthusiasm. But there is no soil of character, and so when the emotions wear off and some difficulty arrives, there is nothing to show for it.*
>
> *The seed cast in the weeds is the person who hears the kingdom news, but weeds of worry and illusions about getting more and wanting everything under the sun strangle what was heard, and nothing comes of it.*

The seed cast on good earth is the person who hears and takes in the News, and then produces a harvest beyond his wildest dreams.

This parable reveals the answer to a secret: why do some reap one hundred-fold, others sixty-fold, and some thirty-fold or nothing at all?

Weeds affect your economy by limiting your harvest. As you pray and read these words, know that the days of missing your harvest or minimizing your harvest are over. With revelation and application comes manifestation.

. . . .

The Farmer

. . . .

The farmer's story is recorded in Matthew 13, Mark 4, and Luke 8. We see that he is sowing good seed. He is sowing in the right season. The problem is not the seed; it is not the season. The problem is the soil!

This soil is full of weeds, and the weeds are choking out the growth of the seed. Jesus is using this natural story to convey a spiritual truth. He tells us that we can know the secrets and the mysteries that surround the growth of the seed, but to the crowds, it was not given. Jesus is careful to give us the information we need— truth is hidden for us, not from us.

We are to study the farmer and understand why our seeds are not producing, whether they are seeds of God's Word or financial seeds into His work. We must be able to discern the weeds we are fighting, and how to destroy them before they destroy our seeds.

America has over nine hundred million acres of farmland. In this country alone, we have about five hundred different varieties of weeds. Each year, three and a half billion dollars are spent on weed killers.

The surprising truth is, there are no weed *killers*. It is a misnomer. The science of weed-killing began in England in the 17th century, with the first products that were advertised to kill weeds. Here in the 21st century, these products have been improved, repackaged, and marketed by Madison Avenue, but they still do not *kill* weeds. They only *control* weeds. If they killed weeds, they would not have to be sprayed continually.

Weed killers only kill the visible part of the weed. The root below ground is still alive. Why is this important? Naturally speaking, it is important because there are roots beneath the surface that allow the weed to grow again and choke out the seed. When the seed is choked out, crops fail. The only successful way to kill weeds is to dig them up completely and destroy the roots.

Spiritually speaking, it is important because people can have mindsets—ways of thinking and believing—that are rooted below the surface. These faulty mindsets will choke the seed before it can grow and produce a harvest.

You must take God's Word and uproot these weeds. I see this frequently. People get in a good church and begin to learn God's principles on seedtime and harvest. For a while, those people will prosper. Then they leave thinking the weeds have been killed. Soon they find out the weeds were just being *controlled* by great faith-building teaching and preaching. When you find a good Church where you are prospering, stay put! Eventually that teaching will uproot those weeds and you will increase as never before in your life!

Never forget how dangerous weeds are to your harvest. Weeds are perennial and only have to be planted one time, and they will come back time after time. Weeds are seeds that contain seeds. Not only do weeds contain seeds, but they also reproduce very quickly once sown. Weeds are seeds planted in the wrong place at the wrong time. Weeds are invasive, unwanted, tenacious, and costly!

. . . .

Seven Truths About Weeds
You Must Never Forget:

. . . .

1. *Weeds produce an abundance of seeds that also produce an abundance of weeds.*
2. *Weeds have an extensive root system and can only be destroyed when the roots are completely eliminated.*
3. *Weeds grow very quickly. In the spring of each year, the weeds are already in the field before the crop seed is even sown.*
4. *Weeds can harbor disease and insects that will rapidly destroy harvests.*
5. *Weeds produce toxic chemicals that will kill vegetables.*
6. *Weeds reduce crop growth. They also determine crop numbers, and they can cause complete crop failure.*
7. *Deadly weeds sometimes produce beautiful flowers, which smell great, but underneath, there is nothing but destruction.*

As you meditate on these seven things, it's easy to see why Jesus told us to study the farmer. A farmer knows about the danger of weeds. Taking a close look, you can see the spiritual application of this parable.

Satan is a liar! We even see him lying to Jesus in the wilderness after Jesus had fasted forty days. As Satan is lying, he is quoting the Word of God to the Son of God. If he is that bold, don't think for a moment that he won't fill a preacher's mouth with lies birthed by religious mindsets to keep you in bondage. Read God's Word for yourself. Don't take my word for it. One would have to be deceived to believe that *seedtime and harvest* is unscriptural.

Matthew 13:24–30 (AMPC) Another parable He set forth before them, saying, The kingdom of heaven is like a man who sowed good seed in his field. But while he was sleeping, his enemy came and sowed also darnel (weeds resembling wheat) among the wheat and went on his way. So when the plants sprouted and formed grain, the darnel (weeds) appeared also. And the servants of the owner came to him and said, Sir, did you not sow good seed in your field? Then how does it have darnel shoots in it?

He replied to them, An enemy has done this. The servants said to him, Then do you want us to go and weed them out? But he said, No, lest in gathering the wild wheat (weeds resembling wheat), you root up the [true] wheat along with it. Let them grow together until the harvest; and at harvest time I will say to the reapers, Gather the darnel first and bind it in bundles to be burned, but gather the wheat into my granary.

This parable is an end-time parable, and one that needs to be taught in every church to all believers today. The *weed* in this parable is *darnel,* called tares in other translations. It is a strong soporific that can strongly affect human behavior, and it can be poisonous in large quantities.

Wheat and darnel look identical when growing together. Darnel is sometimes called false wheat because it so closely resembles wheat. The difference is in the fruit. Wheat can nourish while tares malnourish.

Jesus taught this parable as a last-day warning to His church in order to make them aware of the strong resemblance between truth and error. As I show you the eight characteristics of those who consume tares, I pray your eyes will be opened to see what is going on in the church today.

Are you aware the enemy has come in and divided the body of Christ through the man-made pandemic of COVID-19? We have the virtual church and the actual church; we have the vaccinated church and the unvaccinated church. We have the mega churches and the struggling churches. However, all churches have the same commission from Jesus:

> *Matthew 28:19–20 (KJV) Go ye therefore, and teach all nations, baptizing them in the name of the Father, and of the Son, and of the Holy Ghost: Teaching them to observe all things whatsoever I have commanded you: and, lo, I am with you always, even unto the end of the world. Amen.*

The church of Jesus Christ was birthed into existence on the day of Pentecost (Acts 2). That church was a fire-baptized, apathy-hating, Bible-preaching, sick-healing, devil-defeating group of believers who turned Jerusalem upside down with the gospel. Their altars services brought multitudes into the kingdom of God. People who refused to sow the finances they promised died immediately, and the church continued to grow.

In this parable of the sower, darnel, or tares, represents error; wheat represents truth. As I point out the effects of tares (error) sown amid wheat (truth), I believe it will explain where the church is today!

· · · · · · · · · · · · · ·

Eight Characteristics Of Humans Who Devour Tares

· · · · · · · · · · · · · ·

Darnel's intoxicating properties have been known throughout the ages. It has been used, and misused, for the effects it generates in the human body. One of the reasons it is considered so dangerous, is that if ingested in sufficient quantity, it can kill.

It is easy, as Jesus was doing in this parable, to draw a comparison between darnel and error, between natural effects and spiritual effects. Just as side effects occur naturally with the ingestion of darnel, they also occur spiritually with the ingestion of error. Each of the eight effects darnel has on the human body listed below have parallels in the spiritual experience of Christians. Here are what those effects look like as I have observed them among church people:

1. They become sleepy and drowsy.

In this state, you are no threat to the powers of darkness. This is a restful place, a place where vision is lost. Passion has been replaced by programs. Prophets are now life coaches. Preaching is self-help instead of repentance. Hell has been erased from sermon material. Heaven is seldom talked about. The anti-Christ goes about his business conditioning society for the mark they will soon receive while the pulpit ignores the obvious.

2. They have hypnotic episodes.

Many of us have watched a hypnotist take control of an individual and make them do all sorts of funny things that the person would not normally do. Tares do the same thing when people consume them.

Jesus instructs us that tares are false teachings sown among truth in the last days. These are the last days, without any doubt. The coming of the Lord is at the door.

The greatest orators of my lifetime live at this moment. They can hold a crowd in the palm of their hands with their persuasive style. When a hypnotist snaps his fingers and the person wakes up, he no longer controls them, and they don't realize what has happened.

I have watched worship leaders do the same thing. Once the music has induced a hypnotic state, the people are told to stand, to clap, to dance, and to worship.

Worship is not meant to become a ritual; worship is a lifestyle. Christians should not have to be hypnotized or have their emotions manipulated in order to enter into worship. Worship should flow from a heart of love for Jesus.

3. They enter a state of drunkenness or intoxication.

I don't mean this literally, although it could be taken that way in some churches. Most people have had to deal with a drunk person at some point in their lives. Some are funny; others are obnoxious. All are unproductive. We see them on every street corner in America holding signs that say, "Will work for food."

The food they are talking about comes in a bottle of 90-proof. They live for the next drink that will make them feel good and take their mind off their problems. They are addicted, and they are being controlled by the need for a substance.

I know; I used to be one of them. I know that what they are looking for can't be found at the bottom of a bottle but rather at the foot of the cross. I know this because that's where I found Jesus in a small church on 7th avenue in Chattanooga Tennessee. It was Jesus and the pure Word of God. I was delivered in the church many years ago. I am still delivered.

4. They are unable to walk straight.

The church where I was saved was full of love. They were also full of correction. If you stepped out of line, they were there to put you back in line. They would come back and get you out of your seat, take you to the altar, and pray until devils retreated, and you were revived.

But today, it appears that all lifestyles are acceptable in the culturally correct church. There is little help offered for those who are broken. Altars have been removed or taken from our auditoriums. Altar calls for the lost have been abandoned. Sunday night miracle services are a thing of the past. I can only imagine what a steady diet of tares will produce in the church in the next few years.

5. They have slurred speech.

When you hang out in the lobby of the church and listen to the conversations, it doesn't take long to realize that not many people are talking about the things of God. They talk about everything from Facebook to football. Granted, there is nothing wrong with either of these pastimes. The problem is our church forefathers were talking about Jesus because they feasted on the Word of God and not on the things of the world. In order to follow in their footsteps, we are going to have to change our speech.

Our words order the direction of our lives. Words are seeds that produce a harvest when they are spoken. The reason it's important to not have slurred speech from tares (error) is that we need the truth, the whole truth, and nothing but the truth.

6. They are in a state of stupefaction.

This is the state of being overwhelmed. When a person is extremely drunk, they say they are in a stupor. They don't think straight or act rationally. The least little thing will make a person in this position cry, become depressed, or feel hopeless. This describes many people that I preach to in churches every week.

My heart breaks when they ask for prayer and share their conditions with me around the altar. Tares have poisoned their lives. The least little problems in life devastate them, and they just can't cope. We saw this during the COVID-19 pandemic. People hibernated like hermits. The church where I was saved would have laughed about it. If the government had told them they could not have church, they would have added services. They were full of the Word of God.

7. They are dim-sighted.

Objects appear different when one is inebriated. You can't see clearly or accurately. Hundreds of accidents and even deaths occur each year from drunk drivers. Devouring tares (error) produces the same results in the life of a Christian. Vision is lost, and selfishness and self-preservation replace compassion for the hurting.

People can't see beyond themselves and have little or no regard for anyone else. You work with sinners, live next door to sinners, and are served by sinners at restaurants, grocery stores, and post offices. Do you ever witness to them about the Savior who changed your life?

8. They are apathetic

Apathy can be defined as a lack of interest and a loss of enthusiasm or concern. This defines a lot of Christians and churches today. The church used to be the main focus in most people's lives. Now, there are so many other things that take up their time and capture their interest that the church and the things of God have been relegated to the bottom of the list—if they make the list at all!

It's easy to see, from these eight characteristics of tares, just how efficiently the enemy has sown tares (error) in the church. Knowing this, let me point out a few tares that keep God's people from prosperity. Seedenomics will cause you to prosper economically; weedenomics will cause you to be in lack.

. . . .

Tares Vs. Truth

. . . .

When you compare error (tare) to truth, you can tell the difference by looking at the fruit. Let's look at some of the tares that have been consumed by the church and contrast them with the truth of the Word.

Tare:
Poverty keeps you humble and holy. God is not pleased when one prospers, and Christians should not seek finances.

Truth:
Job 36:11 (KJV) If you obey him you will spend your days in prosperity and your years in pleasure.

Tare:
A rich person cannot be saved or serve God.

Truth:
Genesis 13:2 (KJV) Abraham was very rich in cattle, silver, and gold. Abraham was called the Father of Faith and the friend of God.

Tare:
Prosperity is not for everybody. God wants some to prosper and others to be in lack.

Truth:
Romans 2:11 (KJV) For there is no respect of persons with God.
If God were to prosper one and not the other, He would be a respecter of persons, and His Word would not allow that to come to pass.

Tare:
You should never give expecting anything in return.

Truth:
Luke 6:38 (KJV) Give and it shall be given unto you, good measure, pressed down, shaken together, and running over men will give to your bosom.

. . . .

A Testimony Of Truth

. . . .

When I was preaching on INSP television, a dear African American lady was watching. She didn't normally view preachers who talked about prosperity, but this day she was desperate. Her home of fifteen years was in foreclosure. She had called the mortgage company sixteen times and left messages, but no one would return her call.

I preached that day on sowing a seed that would speak louder than your situation. I related how I had sown a $1,000 seed years prior that had broken the back of debt in my life, enabling me to live debt-free.

She said, "When you finished preaching, I went to the phone and sowed one thousand dollars. The next morning, the mortgage company called me and set up a meeting. This was the same company that had sent me notices saying it was too late to turn things around. Now they wanted to talk to me.

"When we met, the first thing they said was, 'You are not going to lose your house. We will make sure of that.'"

They reduced her payments by over five hundred dollars a month. She is still in that house today. The only thing that changed was that she planted a seed as she was instructed. She sowed that seed and directed it toward a purpose. Her faith and obedience moved the hand of God, and He gave her favor with the mortgage company. What God did for this precious lady, He can do for you, too. Don't allow weedenomics to prevent seedenomics from changing your situation.

Things To Remember From Chapter Seven:

1. There are no such things are weed killers, only weed controllers.

2. Weedkiller only kills the plant on the surface, the root is still alive. You must dig the roots up to kill the weed.

3. Weeds are seeds planted in the wrong place at the wrong time.

4. The difference between wheat and tares is the fruit.

5. Consuming tares will affect your vision and make you drowsy.

6. Tares cause a lack of enthusiasm and concern.

7. Seedenomics will cause you to prosper economically; weedenomics will cause you to lack economically.

CHAPTER 8

The Weeds of Deception

. . . .

Don't be Deceived, Live in Truth

. . . .

The economic structure of the kingdom of God is seedtime and harvest. The problem with the teaching on seedtime and harvest is that it has been mistaught, misrepresented, misunderstood, and misused. The principle has been taken out of context and manipulated for personal gain. The principles of seedtime and harvest are meant to build the kingdom, not divide the kingdom. It is meant to build God's kingdom, not enhance man's kingdom.

In this chapter, I will address the deceptions surrounding seedtime and harvest. I do not want God's people to be without an understanding of everything He has for them. God wants you to prosper. He wants you to prosper so much that He put a spiritual law into place for that purpose:

> *Galatians 6:7 (NKJV) Be not deceived, God is not mocked; for whatever a man sows, that he will also reap.*

We need to get back to this type of teaching in our churches. If we do not teach this generation the principles and the power of sowing and reaping, we will lose the next generation of sowers. It breaks my heart to see ministries and churches shy away from teaching these principles or quit teaching them entirely.

The reason this happens is because they do not want to offend anyone. It is a dangerous thing to teach only part of the Word of God. Preaching based on self-help, self-esteem, affirmation, and positive thinking has a place in the life of a believer, but it must not make us self-sufficient! Remember, God's Word is seed, and seed always produces a harvest. We must teach the whole Bible and not just the parts that are easy on the ears. We must stand with conviction and speak on seedtime and harvest.

We have so many people asking for prayer for their finances when they have been given the answer in the form of a seed. As ministers, we can't be afraid to challenge people to sow when God has already instructed us in His Word to sow. We have a responsibility to share revelation on seedtime and harvest with God's people. If we don't, and we are not deliberate in our teaching and preaching, weeds will appear. They will choke out the Word and make it nonproductive.

We must preach on repentance, conforming to the image of Christ, pursuing the presence of God, faith, miracles, healing, and prosperity. We must preach all of these things; we cannot leave out the preaching on prosperity. If we exclude prosperity, we forfeit our harvest from the seed.

If we preach on all these subjects, we will reap the harvest from the seed. If all our preaching is on self-help, motivation, or becoming a better person, the harvest is a self-sufficient people that only seek God when they have a natural need. Jesus went to great extremes to teach the full gospel. I encourage every teacher and preacher of the gospel today to follow the example of Jesus.

We must be like Jesus and teach what He taught when He was on this earth. The direction of His ministry was seedtime and harvest in every area of life. He dealt with the spiritual, emotional, and material needs of man. This is the reason we must understand seedtime and harvest and how it relates to the *total* man, not just the *material aspect* of man. Sure, we need money, but only if we can be spiritual enough to direct it to God's purpose. We indeed need principles to live a better life as a person, but we also need the anointing and leadership of the Holy Spirit.

If you understand this, it's easy to see why some churches grow and some churches do not. When I refer to church growth, I am not talking about how many people attend that church. That does not constitute a church.

When you look at a cornfield and see the stalks, it's clear that it is a cornfield because it is producing corn. When you look at a church, you can tell it is a church because it is producing souls, miracles, and healings. People are being filled with the Spirit, families are being restored, broken lives are being mended, those in bondage are being released.

Prosperity, peace, and changed lives are the indicators of a real church; crowds are a poor indicator of a real church. If crowds were churches, every sporting event would have a pastor!

If your mind is filled with misconceptions or deceptions about seedtime and harvest, the enemy will come in and interfere with your understanding of prosperity.

To know if we have been a victim of deception, we must first know what *being deceived* means. Being deceived means acting on wrong, improper, or incorrect information. Anytime we step out and place our faith in something that has been said *without first checking the source*, we put ourselves in a position to be deceived.

Deception can be discerned and prevented. Being deceived is an option. As it says in Galatians 6:7, *"Be not deceived…"* The words *"be not"* here indicate that a decision must be made. Some have made the decision to be deceived. This is a dangerous place to be because it will choke out the real Word of God.

Matthew 13:22 (KJV) …the deceitfulness of riches, choke the word, and he becometh unfruitful.

One of the most difficult facts to confront in life is to acknowledge that we have been victims of wrong information. But when the truth does not rule your thoughts and actions, you are deceived. Here is the good news: *you do not have to remain deceived.*

In my own life, I spent several years deceived about prosperity. Having been raised in poverty, I accepted it as a way of life. Then, even after I was born again, my fellow Christians equated spirituality with poverty. The less material things one possessed, the more spiritual he became. With this type of thinking, every impoverished person should have a higher position in the kingdom of God than anyone else.

Nothing is more dangerous than deception that is supported by scriptures that have been taken out of context. It was not until I began to see what Jesus said about wealth, riches, and prosperity that I began to prosper. When we live our lives according to the truth of prosperity, it liberates us from poverty.

Let's look at three major types of deception and the keys to breaking the cycle of deception.

. . . .

Traditional Deception

. . . .

This is a deception that has been passed down from one generation to the next generation without question. This type of deception causes a generational curse. Disobedience to the Word of God re-establishes poverty from one generation to the next until someone believes the truth and breaks the curse.

Let me show you how this deception can be passed down. From the time I was a small child, I was taught that one day, I would grow up and work in the factory where my father and brother worked. On my eighteenth birthday, I was working in the factory at a dead-end job for minimum wage. My family had placed this deception on me. They did not mean to. They are great people who loved me, and they were just passing down the belief that had been instilled in them.

This is happening all over the world today. People are settling and buying into the lie that if their family does not have money, they will not have money. If their family never reached for their dreams, they might as well not even try to reach theirs.

They are teaching the next generation the deception that they were taught. This cycle *must* be stopped, and it *can* be stopped. The generational deception can stop with you.

The way to make this change is the same way I made this change in my own life. When I gave my life to Jesus Christ, I began to read what God's Word said about me. I found out that the Word says I can do all things through Christ. I can rise above my circumstances. The Word of God told me that God wanted me to prosper.

From that time on, I have worked only for myself. I started my own business when I was twenty-three years old, and God caused me to prosper. How did I break the cycle? When my thinking changed, my income changed. So will yours!

. . . .

Doctrinal Deception

. . . .

Most preachers and teachers mean well, but some are seriously misinformed. They don't intend to lead people astray. Many sincere, praying, Godly men and women take a stand against the doctrine of prosperity simply because they have never prospered.

They may also take a stand against prosperity because they have been taught incorrectly. They claim that since Jesus was poor, shouldn't we follow His example and take a vow of poverty? Nothing could be further from the truth!

He was poor in all areas so that we might become rich in all areas. Jesus was also whipped and crucified, but I don't believe God wants us to endure that same treatment. This is just another attempt to enforce the doctrine of poverty over God's people. Let's look at a scripture that contradicts the reason some people think Jesus was poor:

> *2 Corinthians 8:9 (KJV) For ye know the grace of our Lord Jesus Christ, that, though he was rich, yet for your sakes, he became poor, that ye through his poverty might be rich.*

If you use this scripture to support poverty, then you must leave out the last few words of the verse: that you *"might be rich."*

Without the message of prosperity, we could never take the Word of God to the precious souls of this world. Seedenomics is backed by this law.

> Genesis 8:22 (NKJV) *While the earth remains, Seedtime and harvest, Cold and heat, Winter and summer, And day and night shall not cease.*

Seedenomics overrules economics. If it does not, then God is not the God of the supernatural and His Word is not true.

. . . .

Experiential Deception

. . . .

This is thinking produced by what you have already experienced in life. This is based on the lie that your previous experience determines your future expectations. When you buy into this lie, a cycle is created that must be broken. *I am writing this to prophesy that no matter what has happened in the past, it does not have to affect the future.* Today is a brand-new day. Determine in your heart and decree it with your mouth: "Poverty stops with me!"

Don't ever interpret the Word of God based on a previous negative experience. Mindsets are important if we are to prosper.

> *3 John 2 (KJV) Beloved, I wish above all things that thou mayest prosper and be in health, even as thy soul prospereth.*

If we continue to be deceived about prosperity, we will miss out on the blessings that God wants to bring to us. We must break the cycle of deception and step into truth. If we don't, we will be locked into living a limited life.

How To Train A Flea: Take a few fleas and put them in a jar with the lid on. The fleas will attempt to jump out of the jar. Eventually, the fleas will become conditioned to their limitations, and will no longer jump as high as they once jumped. At this point, you can remove the lid and the fleas will remain trapped in the jar. They will jump no higher than the lid. Their offspring will have the same limitations.

A similar process happens in life. After a person experiences failure, defeat, debt, and poverty for a period of time, it becomes a way of life that is seldom questioned. People learn to adjust, and they accept their perceived limits.

I want to challenge you to leap out of your present situation. You are destined for prosperity. Allow your mind to enlarge to a seedenomics mentality—you determine your financial harvest by the seeds you sow.

Do not allow *limitation* to determine *expectation*. Don't let what you *don't have* keep you from what you *can have*. Do not permit fear to fuel your focus. Reach for what seems unattainable. Believe the invisible can become visible.

The Superman Who Could Not Fly: No other story represents the danger of deception like the following story: When I was a boy, the number one program on television was *Superman*.

I remember the day one of my friends came out of the house and told me that he had just watched Superman, and he believed he could fly. I immediately saw an opportunity to have some fun and make some money. I said, "I believe you can fly, too."

I devised a plan. We would tie one of my mom's big towels around his shoulders and make him a cape. Then he would climb up to the peak of the roof on our house. I guess it was about thirty feet from the roof to the ground below. I charged the other kids a quarter to watch my friend fly. I can still see him standing on that roof with the towel flapping in the breeze.

I took a laughing break because I already knew what was going to happen. My friend took off running down the roof, and when he reached the edge, he did a swan dive right out in the air. He flew for about a second, until he hit the ground like a man without a parachute.

We were all rolling in the backyard laughing. I didn't yet know how foolish I had been. The flight almost killed my friend. He broke both arms, cracked several ribs, punctured a lung, and fractured both legs. Why did all this happen? He was a *victim* of deception. I got the worst whipping of my life. I lost a friend but learned a valuable lesson—deception can destroy!

Set The Thermostat A Little Higher: The mind is just like the thermostat in your home. When you want the temperature hotter or colder, you set the thermostat at your desired level. The heating and cooling unit goes to work to change the environment to your expectations. The thermostat has no power to heat or cool on its own, but it is the essential component that directs the heating and cooling unit to produce the desired result.

Our mind has no power to create in and of itself— but it is our thinking that directs our faith. It is impossible to operate in great faith with small thinking.

When, as a young man, I pastored my first church, God began to deal with me about my thinking. After the first year, my church had only increased by about twenty people. I knew God wanted my church to grow, but I had accepted the fact that it would always be small.

Then one day, I walked into the bookstore and saw a book written by Robert Schuller titled *Your Church Has Great Possibilities*. As I began to read this book, my thinking began to increase. I started to tell people that I believed our church would grow, and that eventually, we would have hundreds attending our services. In the next two years, our church added over five hundred new members.

I had the faith for a large church, but my *thinking* had to change so my faith would work at its full potential. You have faith that you will become wealthy. God gave you that faith. But your mind must change so that your faith might attract your increase. Break the cycle by believing that you are a child of increase!

The Chicken In A Duck's World: On a farm in Tennessee, there was a chicken egg that was accidentally placed in a duck's nest. When the little chicken hatched out, he noticed he was different, but he thought he was a duck. The day came when the mother duck took her little ducklings to the pond for their first swim. She walked out across the backyard with her little ones following close behind. When they reached the water, all the little ducks walked right in and began to swim. The little chicken also walked in—but he drowned.

You can see the danger of improper and erroneous thinking in this story. You can drown in debt, lack, want, need, and poverty or you can swim in prosperity and abundance. It depends on your thinking. You do not belong in poverty; you were born again for prosperity. It is only by prospering that you can be an asset to the kingdom of God. It is one thing to pray that people around the world can build churches, schools, hospitals, and orphanages. It is quite another thing when you can write a check and help them do these things.

. . . .

The Weeds Of Deception

. . . .

1 Chronicles 29:12 (NKJV) Both riches and honor come from You, and you reign over all; in your hand is power and might; and in your hand, it is to make great, and to give strength to all.

Hebrews 4:2 (NKJV) But the word which they heard did not profit them, not being mixed with faith in those who heard it.

When our mind rejects the Word of God, faith becomes impossible. Without faith, we can never acquire the prosperity that God desires to give us. Faith creates desire, and desires are essential for increase. *You never acquire what you don't desire, and you never possess what you don't pursue.*

Don't forget that Abraham became rich because his mind took hold of the promises of God, and his faith caused him to obey the instructions God gave him. I can imagine the thoughts that went through his mind: "Play it safe, don't obey God, stay put where you are." Fearful thoughts certainly tried to paralyze his progress, but he continued.

Abraham had to deal with the same thing you deal with when God speaks. Abraham refused to let anything detour his trip down the road of obedience. Abraham had to let the right information prevail over the wrong information. When deception knocked on his door, He sent the truth to answer. You will have to do the same thing.

To uproot the weeds of deception, you are going to have to speak the truth of God's Word. Make flashcards and put them on your mirror if you need to in order to get the Word into your spirit. Take the scriptures from this book and put them before you every day.

Speak words of increase over your life. Speak words of prosperity over your life.

Shut out all the negative words that bombard your mind. Refuse to say, "I can't" or "That's just the way it is." Speak the Word of God over your finances and your life until it changes the way you think, the way you live, and the way you sow.

When you put these keys into practice, your life will be unlocked, and the weeds of deception will be uprooted.

Things To Remember From Chapter Eight:

1. *If we exclude prosperity, we forfeit the harvest from our seed.*

2. *Deception can be discerned and prevented. Deception is an option.*

3. *Nothing is more dangerous than deception that is supported by scriptures that have been taken out of context.*

4. *Deception can be passed down through tradition, doctrine, and experience.*

5. *Don't ever interpret the Word of God based on past negative experiences.*

6. *You will never acquire what you don't desire, and you will never possess what you don't pursue.*

7. *Don't let what you do not have keep you from what you can have. Practice seedenomics instead.*

CHAPTER 9

The Weeds of Voices

Voices That Keep You From Wealth Now

Genesis 3:1 (KJV) "Yea, hath God said, Ye, shall not eat of every tree of the garden?"

In the cool breeze of the morning, the sun slowly rose and pushed back the dark curtain of the night to reveal a clear blue sky. A voice broke the silence of paradise. This voice promised pleasure but could only bring pain. It promised fulfillment, but it left the listener empty. It was the voice of the archangel who rebelled against God and was expelled from the beauty of heaven.

This voice belonged to the one who came to steal, kill, and destroy. Satan told Eve her eyes would be opened, but he failed to tell her that her heart would be broken, her soul would be stained, and paradise would be lost.

A few days before, another voice had spoken to Eve and her husband, but that voice had not appealed to their flesh, but to their spirit. That voice was the voice of God. The devil overheard one part of that conversation:

Genesis 2:16,17 (NKJV) "Of every tree of the garden you may freely eat; but of the tree of the knowledge of good and evil you shall not eat, for in the day that you eat of it you shall surely die."

The Garden of Eden was the crossroads of creation, the very first battlefield of humanity. God's voice was on one side, Satan's on the other, and man was in the middle. The same scene has been repeated for generations. There is the first voice—God. Then the second voice—Satan.

The voice of death and destruction whispers, "Go ahead and eat."

The voice of eternity calls out, "Stop, before it's too late!"

Satan showed Adam and Eve something they could see, while God promised them something they could not see. Satan said, "Go ahead and eat. God's holding out on you. Nothing will happen."

The first choice to obey the voice of a stranger is made, and the result brings sin, sickness, death, and poverty to the entire human race. That voice is still speaking today. Satan's purpose is still the same:

John 10:10 (KJV) The thief cometh not but for to steal, kill, and destroy.

John 8:44 (NIV) For he is a liar and the father of lies.

The young man who wakes up every morning in a cold, gray prison cell on a lumpy mattress heard these lies—the lies that said, "Sell the drugs, rob the convenience store, and take the life of another. You won't get caught; you'll be the one who gets away."

Those lies plant a thought that grows until the mind reaches the point of no return. Satan orchestrates these lies.

These lies convinced my father that his life was not worth living. These lies made him believe that no one loved him or cared for him; he listened to these lies.

One hot June afternoon, I walked through a broken screen door into a small, dark one-room garage apartment. One bed, one lamp, and one chair were arranged around an old wood-burning stove. Except for a few flannel shirts, a couple pairs of overalls, and an old used car, these were the only earthly possessions my 73-year-old father had to show for his life on this earth.

Turning on the light, I sat down in his old brown leather recliner. He had been sitting there just a few hours earlier. Through my tears, I stared at a scene that would be etched into my memory forever. My father had lost his battle with this inner voice. About 1 p.m. on June 25th, he lay down on the floor, took his pistol, placed it between his eyes, and ended his life.

This was one of the darkest days of my life. My dad left no note of farewell or any explanation as to why he had chosen to end his life with his own hands. He left a wife, nine children, numerous grandchildren, and many friends who loved him.

A very dear friend of mine, who is a physician, said something to me that I will never forget. He said, "What your father died from is called a mental malignancy." He compared it to cancer. He explained to me that a mental malignancy is a destructive thought that grows in the mind just like cancer cells grow in the body. He said that once it takes root in the mind, it will continue to grow until the final result is destruction—unless someone can help him remove the thought.

When my friend told me this, I began to understand that this is what the enemy tries to do to every believer. Satan comes and whispers his lies in our ears. He plants thoughts that are diametrically opposed to the voice of God.

Have you heard that voice? That voice proclaims that there is no way out of your situation. That voice declares that God blesses some people, but not everyone. That voice tells you, "Don't tithe, don't sow, just keep what you have. God doesn't expect you to support His work. God doesn't need your money." The lies continue like an endless movie playing on the screen of your mind. If you listen to this voice, you will begin to drift aimlessly on that river of lies.

But I want to tell you that you have a choice. You can believe this voice, or you can believe the truth from the Word of God:

- *What I sow, I will reap (see Galatians 6:7).*
- *If I give, it shall be given to me (see Luke 6:38).*
- *It is God's desire that I prosper (see 3 John 2).*

Which one will you believe? I choose to believe the truth of God's Word. Three voices speak to the sower when he is planting a seed. Two of these voices are weeds, and one is the seed. Which voice are you going to listen to when it comes to sowing and reaping?

. . . .

The Voice of Need

. . . .

When there is a shortage in life, and need is present, there is a voice that begins to speak. It's the same voice Eve heard as she walked that day in Paradise. It is the voice of a weed—the voice of need.

This voice incites fear, doubt, worry, unbelief, panic, and disobedience. This voice is often speaking in the quiet solitude of the late-night hours. The enemy will speak words through the voice of need that are like missiles, aimed at your faith.

I remember hearing this voice one Friday night at 2 a.m. when I found myself in the fight of my life. I had gone to bed after attending a high school football game. I woke up in pain in the middle of the night and was rushed to the hospital. I was dying, and I found myself in surgery. My intestines had shredded in the middle of the night because of stress.

I was pastoring a large church at the time, and it took a toll on my body. A few days later, my doctor, who was also a friend, said, "James, I've done all I can do, and you have at most about a year to live."

As he walked out of the room, I heard the voice of need. "You are going to die! You are going to leave your family in debt with nothing."

When I got out of the hospital, I resigned from my church and went home to die. My vehicles had belonged to the church, so I was left without anything to drive. I had no money in the bank, no way to pay my bills, and I was $247,500 in personal debt and $767,000 in ministry debt. As I lay in my bed, I heard the voice again.

"You are going to lose everything! You and your family will end up homeless! Your ministry is over—there is no way out!" I kept waiting for God to speak, but it seemed like His voice was silent. That is when I realized *I had allowed the voice of need to become louder than the voice of God.*

Once I realized this, and understood the battle I was in, I had to develop a strategy for victory. Victory to me did not include healing at that time. I just didn't want to die defeated. If it was my time to go, I was going to go out fighting.

The first thing I did was get out of bed. This required faith. It was against the doctor's orders. Every victory begins with the first step. After I showered and dressed, I felt like going back to bed, but I refused to give in to my body.

I called a friend, borrowed a vehicle, and booked a preaching engagement in a small church in Oklahoma. The voice of need continued to scream, but I refused to listen. I would say, "Shut up, Devil, in the name of Jesus!"

I would not be writing these words today if I had given in to that voice. I had made up my mind that day that the voice of need would not speak louder than the voice of God in my life. When you are faced with a need, you are faced with a choice. You can give in to the voice of need, or you can start speaking the Word of God over your situation. You can focus on your needs, or you can plant a seed. *When you plant a seed in a time of need, you get God's attention.* Don't let the voice of need speak louder than the voice of God in your life.

· · · · · · · · · · · · ·

The Voice of Greed

· · · · · · · · · · · · ·

The voice of greed, also a weed, appeals to your sense of security. It says, "Hold on to what you have. If you release it, you will have nothing."

The truth is, "When you hold on to what you have, that's all you will ever have."

When I received my first offering in that little church in Oklahoma, my needs were so great that I looked at the offering and the mountain of bills, and I felt hopeless.

Then I heard the voice of God. He said, "Plant a seed to meet your need."

Then greed spoke, "Keep everything, you need it."

At that moment I was determined to sow my way out of my situation. I needed money, so I would sow money. I planted that seed in obedience, praying that God would use it to create what I needed. I needed God to break the spirit of debt and disease. If He didn't, I was not going to make it.

I made up my mind that what I had in my hand was not enough to meet my needs, so I must plant it as a seed. When I did, God was faithful to meet me at my point of commitment. From the moment I released that seed, I started expecting in faith for my debt to be erased and miracles to be released.

Not only did I expect, but I also began to keep track of my seeds. When I planted a seed, I entered it into my prayer journal, and I put the date I planted it beside the amount. Then, I would pray over the seed.

As I continued to sow, God began to multiply my seed. When the harvest would come in, I would sow more and use what was left to pay my creditors. The year the doctor had told me I would live began to draw to a close, and I was still extremely sick and still very much in debt. I had to sell everything I could live without, and I did not seem to be making very much progress. I had made up my mind that I was going to trust God with my finances and not hold on to what He was instructing me to release. I was not going to let greed speak louder than my seed.

. . . .

The Voice Of Your Seed

. . . .

God gives us seed to sow. That seed is in the form of money.

Ecclesiastes 10:19 (NKJV) A feast is made for laughter, And wine makes merry, But money answers everything.

This one verse tells us our seed has a voice. Our seed will speak to our need and call forth our harvest. Our seed will speak to our needs. When a natural seed is sown, the soil calls forth the nutrients to come and produce a harvest. The same is true with a spiritual seed. When a seed is planted in the spiritual realm, the voice of God speaks to the seed to bring forth. When that Word is heard, the seed begins to heat up and breaks open for multiplication. The voice of the seed speaks multiplication into action.

Satan knows this, so he always tries to speak when the voice of the seed is speaking. He tries to cancel the seed's assignment by making you listen to his voice and not the seed's voice.

If you do hear the voice of the seed but fail to sow, then you will still be defeated. But if you listen to the voice of the seed and sow, you will prosper. The voice of the seed says, "If you sow, you will reap. The more you sow, the more you will reap." Listen to the voice of the seed.

There is more to my story. The year the doctors told me I would live was almost over—I had five days left. It looked as if I would die in the bondage of debt. All I could think about was the widow in 2 Kings 4. Her husband died, leaving her with the children, no money, and a stack of bills.

I knew this story, and I knew that this was not God's will for my life. I needed an answer. I needed prosperity now! I had no more revivals scheduled to preach, and only $1,000 to last me for the next month. When I went to the church where I was speaking on Sunday morning, God spoke to me. He did not say what I wanted to hear. He said, "Give that $1,000 in the offering today and trust me." At this moment, the other voices began to speak. The battle was raging.

We wrote the check that day and placed it in the offering. We left with no money. We were on the road—with no money to eat lunch and no way to pay our motel bill. It was a dark day! My faith was on the line. My wife, my son, and I began to pray.

After a little while, they took a nap, and I continued to talk to God. Just as I was telling Him I had done all I could do, there was a knock on the door. It was a man from the church. He said the pastor sent him to see if I could begin a revival that night. He continued to tell me that they had paid my motel bill through the week, and they had made arrangements for meals at the restaurant next door. Then, he handed me a check. I put the check in my pocket. As I talked with him, I tried to feel the numbers on the check. I was anxious to see the amount, but I did not want to appear obvious. When the man left, I opened the check, and it was $1,500. Praise God!

But that's not the best news! God healed me instantly! I preached a three-week revival for the church, and we had over three hundred conversions.

Over the next twelve months, God helped me get out of debt. Now, thirty-four years have passed, and I am still operating my personal life and my ministry debt-free. The church where I conducted this meeting was one of the first churches where we raised money and paid off the church mortgage. If I had not obeyed God that day, you would not be reading these words, and that church would not be debt-free.

. . . .

Debt-Free Living

. . . .

In the last thirty-four years, we have helped hundreds of people and a great number of churches become debt-free. I was preaching in a church that was meeting in an industrial center and saving money to get their own building. They had saved up $8,800. They had found some older buildings, but no financial institution would loan them any money.

The second week of my preaching there, the pastor and board decided to sow that $8,800 into our ministry. It was very humbling to me. I took that seed, and we prayed for a building. Six months after I left that church, the pastor called me. He told me an unbelievable story.

He said he had received a call two weeks prior from an older pastor who was retiring. He had a building that would seat around seven hundred people. It had a family life center and a school, and it was sitting on fifteen acres right on a major interstate! This church was seen daily by hundreds of thousands of people. The retiring pastor told my friend that the Lord had spoken to him to give him the building, and their people would merge with his people. A few weeks later, we went back and dedicated this building debt-free to my friend's congregation. This is the power of a seed!

As you read these words, the devil will make you think that this could never happen in your life. Let me ask you: why not? God does not have favorites. God is moved by faith. The greatest expression of faith is a seed sown into the work of God. God changed my life with a seed. He changed the church by a seed. If you listen to the Holy Spirit, He will lead you to sow a seed that will change your life.

In fact, as you read these words, I believe that God is dealing with you about a certain seed that you need to sow. It is a seed you have never sown before—it will stretch your faith. It will cause your heart to beat faster as you write the check. How do I know this? I have been there.

I just wrote a $10,000 check this morning to sow into Christian television. I am believing God for a $100,000 harvest. I have some things I want to do for missions. I also just wrote a check yesterday to help build a church in India. Last week, we wrote a check to buy two hundred chairs for a church in Kenya.

The reason God wants to bless us is so that we can be a blessing. This is the benefit of debt-free living. When God speaks, you can respond without hesitation to be a blessing. If you just want to be blessed, you are not a candidate for abundance. The way God gets money into the kingdom to further the gospel is through people He can trust to sow finances. If we sow what is in our hands into God's work, He will sow what is in His hands into our world.

A couple wrote me a letter and asked me to pray that they could get out of debt. They sent a generous seed along with their letter. They had $90,000 in credit card debt, a mortgage, and two car payments. I laid their letter on my altar, and I began to pray for them each day. In just a few weeks, the company the man worked for asked him to move to one of their other locations in another state. They told him they would pay off all his credit card debt, furnish him a house, and give him a company car. In a matter of weeks, this couple was living in another state that they love, and they were enjoying a debt-free life. Again, we can see the power of the seed.

. . . .

Which Voice Will You Listen To?

. . . .

When you are faced with a situation that seems insurmountable, it is vital that you listen to the right voice. You can allow the voice of need or greed to stop you from sowing a seed that will release prosperity. Every seed comes with a choice. You can sow or you can hold. What you hold on to will never grow.

Some of you are reading this, and you want to sow, but the *voice of need* is saying, "You can't afford to sow."

Maybe you are hearing the *voice of greed* that is saying, "You need that money; you better hold on to it."

All the while, the *voice of the seed* is saying, "God will provide."

I want to encourage you to remember that God provides seed for the sower. God will provide for a *sower*, not for a *hoper*. Make up your mind to be a sower. God is not holding up your harvest. *The seed in your hand that has not been planted is delaying your harvest.*

God wants to meet every one of your needs. But I learned a long time ago, God is moved to compassion by my need, but He is moved into action by my faith. When I move out in faith and sow a seed, God meets me at my point of faith. He speaks to me and gives me an opportunity to sow. God is not obligated to me past the point of opportunity. What happens in terms of harvest is directly related to what voice I listen to in my life.

The voice you listen to and follow determines every outcome in your life. It determines your destiny. You are where you are today because of the voices you have obeyed. God will always lead you to a life of abundance, and Satan will lead you down a road of lack. You need to silence the wrong voices today and listen to the right voice. When God is speaking to you about a seed, listen and obey.

Things To Remember From Chapter Nine:

1. *The voice of need speaks to produce fear, doubt, worry, unbelief, panic, and disobedience.*

2. *Don't let the voice of need speak louder than the voice of God in your life.*

3. *What you hold on to is all that you will ever have. A seed will only increase when it is released.*

4. *Plant a seed to meet your need.*

5. *The voice of the seed speaks multiplication into action. It calls a harvest into fruition.*

6. *God is moved by faith, not favorites.*

7. *When God speaks to you about a seed, don't hesitate—be obedient and sow!*

PART IV

SEEDONOMICS MENTALITY

· · · · · ·

CHAPTER 10

Five Characteristics of Sowers

. . . .

A Sower Loves To Sow And Lives To Sow!

. . . .

2 Corinthians 9:10–11 (AMPC) And [God] Who provides seed for the sower and bread for eating will also provide and multiply your [resources for] sowing and increase the fruits of your righteousness [which manifests itself in active goodness, kindness, and charity]. Thus you will be enriched in all things and in every way so that you can be generous, and [your generosity as it is] administered by us will bring forth thanksgiving to God.

2 Corinthians 9:10–11 (MSG) This most generous God who gives seed to the farmer that becomes bread for your meals is more than extravagant with you. He gives you something you can then give away, which grows into full-formed lives, robust in God, wealthy in every way so that you can be generous in every way, producing with us great praise to God.

It was about 3 a.m. when I woke up in a hotel room in Sugarland, Texas. I had been sleeping for about 4 hours. As I wiped the sleep from my eyes, I saw a beam of light coming in my window from the outside. It was shining on the yellow legal pad that is always on the nightstand beside my bed.

As I was looking at that beam of light, I heard a voice inside me say, "Get your pen and pad. I want to give you the characteristics of a sower." I began to write as quickly as I could.

When I finished, I realized that this must be important, so I said aloud, "Why do I need to recognize sowers?

Then I heard this: "Because when you sow into non-sowers, your harvest stops there." Needless to say, I was fully awake at this point!

The Bible tells us that God gives seed to the sower. If you have no seed, you either ate your seed or you are not a sower. Every harvest has seeds for eating and seeds for sowing. Since God promised seed to the sower—and that He would multiply the seed sown—we need to recognize sowers. God showed me certain characteristics that would help me recognize a sower when I met them.

God had spoken something so profound that it arrested my attention as I lay there in those quiet hours of the morning, I reminisced about all the non-sowers I had sown into over the years. I received the revelation that when you sow seed into non-sowers it ends the potential of that seed because the seed will be eaten.

Some soil is not capable of producing a good harvest. The level of harvest is in the soil. If the soil is not good, it can trap the destiny of the seed. At that moment, I immediately repented and promised the Lord I would never sow into another non-sower if He would help me.

I said, "Lord, help me be able to distinguish a sower from a non-sower. Do not let me sow based just on emotions another day of my life."

Have you ever heard a sad story that moved you to sow emotionally? Maybe you heard a testimony that moved you to sow a seed emotionally. You sowed with two different types of emotions, but you reaped the same types of harvest: nothing.

What the Holy Spirit was impressing upon me was that He is the only one I should listen to when it comes to sowing. It is the Holy Spirit who will direct me to the right place at the right time to maximize my harvest! I can't let emotions override the guidance of the Holy Spirit.

As God began to speak, I began to write. Here is what the Lord gave me that day about the traits of a sower:

. . . .

Sowers Sow:
The Buzzards, Boulders, and the Briars!

. . . .

Matthew 13:3–8 (AMPC) And He told them many things in parables (stories by way of illustration and comparison), saying, A sower went out to sow. And as he sowed, some seeds fell by the roadside, and the birds came and ate them up. Other seeds fell on rocky ground, where they had not much soil; and at once they sprang up because they had no depth of soil.

But when the sun rose, they were scorched, and because they had no root, they dried up and withered away. Other seeds fell among thorns, and the thorns grew up and choked them out. Other seeds fell on good soil, and yielded grain—some a hundred times as much as was sown, some sixty times as much, and some thirty.

We can see in this portion of scripture a sower going out to sow. We also see that not all the seeds that he sowed produced a harvest. Still, he continued to sow.

This is a valuable lesson to learn—we grow as we sow! In other words, as we continue to sow, we get better at discerning where to sow and how to sow. I have talked to people who sowed seeds and did not get a harvest. They gave up and said, "This sowing and reaping is not of God."

When seeds do not produce a harvest, it's not God's doing. Often, it usually is the soil that was chosen. Another reason could be that the seed was stolen before it had the chance to produce a harvest.

In this parable, for example, the buzzards, the boulders, and the briars got some of the seed before it could produce a harvest. But the sower still continued to sow!

For the last forty-six years of my life, I have been a sower—both naturally and spiritually. Until a few years ago, I lived on a forty-acre farm. Each year, I sowed a garden. We canned the vegetables for the winter the way we did when I was growing up.

One year, I wanted to get an early start with the garden because I was going to be traveling a lot. So, I sowed a month early. About the time the plants were coming out of the ground, we had a frost and it killed everything I had sown.

So, what did I do? Did I curse the seed and say, "I give up on farming"? No, I did not give up on farming. I just learned from my mistake. I went out and bought some more seeds and sowed again. I had a great crop that year.

In the natural, I have sown seeds that did not produce a harvest into certain ministries. Unfortunately, there are some churches and organizations that do not use money properly. Some abuse money and are not good stewards, or they use it selfishly.

I have sown into ministries that have large debts. Whenever I sowed into this type of soil, I did not get a harvest. I have learned through the years to only sow where, when, and how the Holy Spirit leads me to sow. He knows more than I do about good ground and poor ground.

A sower can't help but sow. It is in their blood. They live to sow. Before I was a Christian, I was addicted to drugs and alcohol. That is all I lived for in my life. I had to have them every day. Well, the Lord said to me one day "If you will become addicted to sowing, I will help you support your habit." I did, and He has! I live to sow! I wake every morning thinking about where I can sow that day.

God did not promise seed to the person who prays. To them, He promised power. He did not promise seed to the person who praises. To them, He promised His presence. He only promised to give seed to the sower!

. . . .

Sowers See:
They Can See The Harvest In The Seed.
They Can See The Seed In The Harvest.

. . . .

There is a difference between a sower and someone who sows occasionally. A true sower can tell you that certain tomato plants can produce hundreds of tomatoes per season. They also know that there are approximately twenty-five seeds in each tomato. If the plant produces two hundred tomatoes, this equals about five thousand seeds per season from the one seed that was planted.

A sower sees because he has revelation knowledge. This comes through experience. In the natural, a beginning sower is given a picture of the product he is sowing on the front of the package. I learned this from my mom, who taught me about sowing.

She would take a stick and put it at the beginning of a row of corn, cucumbers, carrots, or beans. Then, she would take the seed packet with the picture on it and put it on the stick. This way she had a picture of her harvest before it ever broke through the earth. When you looked at that picture you knew that *what you could visualize would soon materialize.*

In the kingdom of God, Jesus spent hours teaching on seedtime and harvest. He continually used agricultural metaphors to create sowers and help them see the results of sowing seeds.

He taught that a man who sowed seed went to bed and when he woke up, he had a harvest and did not know how it happened. All this teaching was to raise up sowers who could see the harvest in the seed and the seed in the harvest.

After many years of sowing, I have become a hundredfold sower. I was not always at this level. This came through trial and error, and many years of study on seedtime and harvest. One day, I made up my mind that if anyone was going to reap a hundredfold, it might as well be me.

For my seed to produce at this level, I had to make sure I was sowing in good ground. The most productive ministry ground for me was Christian television. Each time I would sow into this media, I would get a quick, hundredfold harvest. I believe the hundredfold return is the maximum harvest possible from a seed. It is not one hundred times—it's one hundredfold.

When I opened my eyes to this revelation, I could begin to identify the increase. It always came back in the form of provision and prosperity. Sometimes, the harvest would be tires on the vehicle lasting longer, utility bills that were suddenly cheaper, better gas mileage, overtime at work. God touched normal everyday things and brought in the harvest.

. . . .

Sowers Know:
If They Don't Sow In Tough Times,
They Won't Reap In Good Times!

. . . .

Jesus taught in Matthew 6 that good times and bad times come to both the saint and the sinner. We do not believe for bad times, but they come as a fact of life. We cannot prevent bad times, but we can determine how they affect us by the seeds we sow during this time.

It is essential when we walk through tough times that we continue to sow the Word of God by speaking it. Instead of giving verbal attention to the problem, we speak the Word to our problems. Does this mean we deny there is a problem? Of course not! We just do not focus on the problem. We continue to speak the Word of God.

Romans 10:17 (NKJV) Faith comes by hearing, and hearing by the word of God.

Remember that fear comes the same way faith comes. Both faith and fear come by hearing. If we are speaking negatively, it will affect the outcome of a situation. If you do not believe this, go out to eat with four or five people at a place that only serves fish. After everyone gets their order, take one bite, push your plate back and say, "This tastes funny. I heard that some people have been dying from fish that has too much mercury." I promise you that there will be a lot of fish left on the table. The words that you have spoken will produce fear in the hearer.

A study of history tells us of the one hundred and two people who boarded a boat in 1620 and sailed across the ocean to escape the persecution of King James and to have the freedom to worship God. Their journey was a grueling ten weeks at sea.

They drafted a document called the Mayflower Compact that would establish a self-governing colony where they could freely worship God together.

The pilgrims reached shore in November and that first winter almost half of them died due to starvation and extreme cold temperatures. By spring, those who remained were severely rationing their last corn in order to survive. These were the toughest of times.

It was then they decided to take the corn that remained and sow it in a small parcel of ground. One year after they had come to America, they reaped their first harvest, and the ones who remained—along with the native Americans who had taught them to plant corn and hunt game—celebrated for three days, which was the first Thanksgiving! They sang, read scripture, and worshipped God together. But what if they had not sown in tough times? Would we have the affluent nation we have today?

. . . .

Sowers Reap:
A Sower Reaps Exactly What He Sows!

. . . .

Galatians 6:7–9 (MSG) What a person plants, he will harvest. The person who plants selfishness, ignoring the needs of others—ignoring God! harvests a crop of weeds. All he'll have to show for his life is weeds! But the one who plants in response to God, letting God's Spirit do the growth work in him, harvests a crop of real life, eternal life. So let us not allow ourselves to get fatigued from doing good. At the right time, we will harvest a good crop if we do not give up or quit.

In the kingdom of God, and in the teachings of Jesus as well as the Apostle Paul, you see that the same thing is true. Whatever you sow, you will reap. If you sow selfishness, you harvest weeds. That is the fruit of selfishness.

Not every seed sown is planted in the same type of soil. I have seen some people who started off sowing in sincerity and over time started sowing in selfishness. They could not figure out why they began reaping selfishness, and I had to explain to them that it was because they were simply reaping what they had sown.

A man came to talk to me about his financial situation. He and his wife were in their mid-forties, and they were living in a six hundred-square-foot garage apartment and working for minimum wage. He told me that he had just enrolled in a school and was pursuing a new career. He told me that if I would pray for his success, he would sow a 10% tithe and a 10% seed to the church from each paycheck.

We knelt for prayer in my office, and I asked God to anoint this man and bless him. Before long, he brought me a tithe of fifty dollars and a seed of fifty dollars. This continued to grow, and God blessed this man. One day, he made an appointment and wanted to talk about his commitment.

By this time, he and his wife were driving a Mercedes and building a beautiful new custom home in an exclusive community. He had begun to miss church on Sundays. As he sat on the other side of my desk, he said, "Pastor, I cannot keep my commitment any longer. I made one million dollars this month, and my tithe would be one hundred thousand and my seed would be one hundred thousand.

I said, "Brother, that will be no problem."

He said, "I was praying that you would be understanding."

I said, "Let's kneel here and pray." I begin to pray, "God, please take your anointing off this man, and let him get back to an amount where he can be obedient to you in his sowing."

He jumped up from prayer and screamed, "Don't pray that prayer! Give me a pen!" He quickly wrote out two one hundred-thousand-dollar checks and said, "You won't have any more problems with me." I had moved him from selfishness back to sincerity. God continued to bless him.

The reason God cannot bless some people as He wants to bless them is that they become selfish. The scriptures also tell us that we are to listen and be led by the Holy Spirit in our sowing. The purpose of abundance is to be able to care for your family and be a blessing to the work of God. No one, not even a preacher, is immune to selfishness.

I have observed men and women of God over the years who rose from poverty to great prosperity. Their lifestyles changed dramatically. When they stood to preach, they equated their position with God by their assets. While there is absolutely nothing wrong with anyone having great wealth, we must be on guard that wealth does not have control of us.

When God asks you to do something for His kingdom and you cannot respond, you should realize you are no longer serving God— you are serving the money your seed produced. As we prosper, we will be tested in these areas.

. . . .

Sowers Stand:
There Is A Battle Between Seedtime
And Harvest!

. . . .

A farmer battles insects, weather, and weeds every time he sows a seed. He is a fighter. He is prepared for obstacles. He is armed with weed killer, insect spray, and prayer. He can control the bugs and the weeds, but he needs God to help him with the weather.

We can learn a lot from the farmer when it comes to our financial harvest. The battle begins the moment the seed is sown. In the parable of the sower in Matthew 13, the birds came immediately to steal the seed and prevent the harvest.

Since there is a period between seedtime and harvest, we need to be patient—we must wait. We battle impatience, along with doubt, fear, unbelief, weariness, and the temptation to give up and quit.

> *James 5:7 (KJV) Be patient, therefore, brethren, unto the coming of the Lord. Behold, the husbandman waiteth for the precious fruit of the earth, and hath long patience for it, until he receives the early and latter rain.*

In the Old Testament, there is a story that illustrates the battle that surrounds harvest. Each year when the Israelites were getting close to harvest, the Philistines would sit upon the hillside and wait until the fruit was ready to gather. Then, they would come down off the hillside, the Israelites would flee, and they would take the harvest.

Does this sound familiar? Have you lost harvest the same way? The Philistines took the harvest without a fight until one day, things changed. A man named Shammah got tired of losing his harvest. He said, "Enough is enough! I would rather die fighting than live fleeing! He stood his ground.

2 Samuel 23:11-12 (AMPC) Next to [Eleazar] was Shammah son of Agee the Hararite. The Philistines were gathered at Lehi on a piece of ground full of lentils; and the [Israelites] fled from the Philistines. But he stood in the midst of the ground and defended it and slew the Philistines, and the Lord wrought a great victory.

These verses tell us that Shammah stood, and God fought his enemy. When *he* did what he could do, *God* did what he could not do.

Are you tired of almost getting what you need? You are a sower, but every time you sow, all hell breaks loose against you. Can I encourage you to take a stand? Stand on the Word of God and begin to declare and decree it. Tell your enemy, "I am not losing another harvest!"

If you are facing a battle you have never faced, it is only because you are close to a breakthrough you have never experienced! The bigger the blessing, the fiercer the conflict—but you will win if you don't quit.

Sowers do not quit, sowers sow! Sowers sow in the good times and the bad times. Sowers always look for a place to sow. Sower's sow what they want to reap. Sowers see the harvest in the seed and the seed in the harvest. Make up your mind today that with God's help, you are going to become a sower who will change this world. The first step to becoming a sower is to make up your mind that you will sow every time the Holy Spirit leads you to sow. You will not try to negotiate with God, but you will always sow exactly what He leads you to sow.

Things To Remember From Chapter Ten:

1. *Some soil is not capable of producing a good harvest.*

2. *A sower loves to sow and lives to sow.*

3. *A sower can see the harvest in the seed and the seed in the harvest.*

4. *Faith comes by hearing; fear also comes by hearing.*

5. *The reason God cannot bless some people the way He wants to is because they have become selfish.*

6. *If you are facing a battle you have never faced, it is only because you are close to a breakthrough you have never experienced!*

7. *Sowers do not quit. Sowers sow!*

CHAPTER 11

Five Reasons to Sow in Tough Times

In the natural, the seed has to wait on the right season, but in the kingdom, the right season is waiting on the seed!

> *Psalm 126:4–6 (NLT) Restore our fortunes, Lord, as streams renew the desert. Those who plant in tears will harvest with shouts of joy. They weep as they go to plant their seed, but they sing as they return with the harvest. Turn to freedom our captivity and restore our fortunes, O Lord, as the streams in the South (the Negeb) [are restored by the torrents].*
>
> *They who sow in tears shall reap in joy and singing. He who goes forth bearing seed and weeping [at needing his precious supply of grain for sowing] shall doubtless come again with rejoicing, bringing his sheaves with him.*

The Psalmist wrote these words in extremely difficult times. I am sure you can relate to his lament! There are times in our lives when it is not easy to sow the seeds God is asking us to sow. We must remember that the harvest is always bigger than the seed. God will lead us to plant our greatest seed when we have our greatest need.

. . . .

Sowing In A Famine

. . . .

In Genesis 26, there was a famine in the land—as bad as the famine during the time of Abraham.

> *Genesis 26:1-2 (KJV) And there was a famine in the land, other than the former famine that was in the days of Abraham. And Isaac went to Gerar, to Abimelech king of the Philistines.*
>
> *And the Lord appeared to him and said, Do not go down to Egypt; live in the land of which I will tell you.*

God was telling Isaac not to run from his difficulties but to stay in the land and He would bless him. The word *bless* here means to empower, excel, increase, rise above, and prosper. It also means to make more of you than you currently are at this moment. He told Isaac, "I will lift you to a new level." Has God ever spoken to you to stay in the place where He sent you and He will bless you? I know He has said that to me.

He told Isaac, "I will give all the land to you and your children." When God gives you a direction, your answer not only affects you, but it will also affect your family for generations. God told Isaac that He would make his descendants as many as the stars in the sky, and He would give them all the land. He promised Isaac that all the nations of the earth would get a blessing through his descendants.

This sounds like an awesome deal for Isaac. He and his descendants will be blessed, and all the nations will be blessed through them. The reason God was going to bless Isaac was because of the covenant his father had made and kept with God.

In Genesis 26, we see Isaac in the middle of the famine wanting to pack up and move. Have you ever been going through so much turmoil that you wanted to pack up and go somewhere else? Instead, he chose to remain and planted crops in that land. The harvest from those seeds was huge. God had kept his promise and blessed Isaac.

Seeds sown in times of devastation produce maximum multiplication. It says that Isaac became richer and richer by the day until he was very wealthy. He accumulated flocks and herds and many, many servants. He amassed so much wealth that the Philistines began to envy him. Isaac, in a time of famine, obeyed the voice of the Lord and sowed and reaped a huge harvest.

Five things that happened to Isaac because he sowed in tough times are recorded in Genesis 26.

➤ He waxed great (v. 13)
➤ He went forward (v. 13)
➤ He grew until he became very great (v. 13)
➤ He had possession of flocks, herds, servants (v.14)
➤ He was envied by his enemies (v.14)

If these things happened for Isaac through his obedience to sow in tough times, I know it can happen for all of God's people. We can learn a lesson from Isaac in this passage.

. . . .

Five Reasons To Sow In Tough Times

. . . .

#1: Your seed gives birth to expectation and attracts what is necessary for your harvest.

You only attract what you expect. If you are not expecting anything, don't be surprised that you are not attracting anything. It takes a seed to activate the law of attraction. Just like the seed attracts the nutrients from the soil that are needed for harvest, your expectation attracts your harvest. My friend, Dr. Rod Parsley, says that *the atmosphere of expectancy is the breeding ground for miracles.* I agree with this statement. Seed activates expectation and attracts the harvest in tough times. In tough times, a lot of people lose sight of this principle, when it is this very principle that can bring them a breakthrough.

#2: If you don't sow when things are tough, you will not reap even when things are better.

If your seed remains in your hand, then your harvest remains in God's hand. God *orchestrates* your harvest, but your seed *initiates* your harvest. God will not do *anything* until you do *something.* Isaac learned this principle: when he sowed, God moved. We have a generation that wants God to move and *then* they will sow. If God moved before we sowed, we would never sow. It takes faith to sow and wait for God to move.

If God sent the rain before the seed, it would just get the soil wet! It would not cause multiplication. With no seed to water, there would be no harvest to reap. Isaac had to sow *before* the rain so that when the rain came, it would ignite the seed and produce a huge harvest.

Isaac did not wait until times were better. He sowed in the season God spoke to him to sow, and he reaped a harvest.

#3: Seed overcomes world conditions.

> *Ecclesiastes 11:4–6 (NKJV) He who observes the wind will not sow, And he who regards the clouds will not reap. As you do not know what is the way of the wind, Or how the bones grow in the womb of her who is with child, So you do not know the works of God who makes everything. In the morning sow your seed, and in the evening do not withhold your hand; For you do not know which will prosper, Either this or that, Or whether both alike will be good.*

Seeds are not moved by political problems, religious compromise, or even pandemics. Seeds are designed to multiply and bring forth a harvest—and that is what they do. A farmer can die, and his seed will still produce a harvest. It doesn't matter what the conditions of the world are, you can still sow and reap. You can sow in famine and reap a hundred-fold. How does this happen?

I was recently in Lagos, Nigeria with my dear friend and mighty man of God, Pastor Chris Oyakhilome. Pastor Benny Hinn, Bishop Clarence McClendon, and Bishop Dan Willis were also there. We were attending a birthday party for Pastor Chris. It was one of the most glorious events I have ever experienced.

Pastor Chris is the most anointed apostle I've met in my forty-six years of full-time ministry. As we sat and talked with him, I could only compare it to what it must have been like to visit with the Apostle Paul. His wisdom, love, generosity, and compassion touched me deeply. We were going to have three services, from Monday through Wednesday, to allow partners to sow into the Love World Television Network.

When I woke up on Monday morning, the Lord did not even say, "Good morning." He said, "I want you to sow $10,000 today into Love World Television." His word was so clear. When God speaks a large amount that doesn't fit into my budget, I want to make sure it is Him. As I was pondering this, the Lord spoke one of the greatest revelations He has ever spoken to me about seedtime and harvest.

As I was preparing my check, I looked down on my desk and saw the package of corn seeds that I carry with me to use for illustration. It was facedown, and there was a map of the United States on the back. Printed beside the map were the dates for the different growing seasons across the country.

As I looked at it, the Lord spoke to me and said: "*In the natural, the seed has to wait on the right season; in the kingdom, the right season is waiting on the seed!*"

I had never heard anyone say that. I said, "Lord, are you saying that my season of harvest is waiting on my seed?

He said, "Yes!"

I planted my seed that morning, and God opened the windows of heaven over my finances. Before December came to an end, God had supplied my complete budget for the next year. I am so glad I didn't miss my opportunity!

If you are going through a season of debt, financial lack, oppression, family problems, divorce, disease, or difficulty, you can change that season with a seed. As you sow, your season will change. Sowing is the greatest expression of faith. Sowing can change a famine into the right season.

#4: Faith is magnified in tough times.

The story in Mark 12 demonstrates the kind of faith that we must display in tough times. This story is about a widow with two mites. This was all the money that she had; this was her livelihood. It says that Jesus sat and watched as the people came and gave. He saw rich people put in a lot of money, and then He saw the widow put in two mites. He called the disciples over to teach them a lesson about giving. He told them that this poor widow had given more than anyone else.

I'm sure the disciples looked confused after seeing the large gifts that the rich were giving. Jesus said, "They were giving out of their abundance, but she was giving out of her lack. She had given the most because she gave all she had."

In tough times, you must be willing to give it all if He asks for it all. I want you to understand this principle: *Faith is determined by what you have left, not by what you released!*

#5: Refusing to sow now disqualifies you from your future harvest.

God promises to multiply seeds that are sown. Every seed has within it the potential for harvest. God spoke it into the seed. However, for that potential to be released, the seed must be sown and connected with the proper soil. Seeds will produce a harvest if they are planted in the right place at the right time. The problem is that we don't plant in tough times, so when times improve, we don't reap.

We can't spend our lives searching for a harvest when we have not planted seeds. That is like going to the ATM to make a withdrawal without ever having made a deposit. The moment of increase begins after the moment of release. If you are going to see a harvest in the future, you must plant seeds now. *Tomorrow's harvest is in today's seed.*

Many people eat their seeds during tough times out of disobedience. It's not that God isn't asking them to sow; they are just not listening. They want to do better; they want to be obedient. However, disobedience wins because of their need.

> *Isaiah 1:19 (KJV) "If you be willing and obedient, you shall eat the good of the land.*

It takes more than a willing heart; it takes an obedient hand to sow a seed in tough times. For every act of disobedience, there is a consequence. If you choose to eat your seed instead of sowing it, you disqualify yourself from that potential harvest.

Some seeds, if eaten, will make you sick. Some seeds are even poisonous! Apple seeds, peach pits, and cherry pits are toxic. They contain cyanide. If you consume enough of them, they will kill you. There are some seeds that you can't eat. There's a difference between seeds for eating and seeds for sowing. I have found out…

- *When you eat seeds meant for sowing, they will leave a bad taste in your mouth.*
- *Seeds meant for sowing can produce a harvest if sown or death if eaten!*

The lesson here is to *never eat what is supposed to be sown.* Eating your sowing seed will not result in a harvest, it will only lead to lack. Make sure you do not eat what God is asking you to sow. Don't disqualify your seed because of disobedience. Listen to the Holy Spirit, and sow when you are led to sow.

. . . .

Difficult Seeds In Desperate Times

. . . .

As I worked to become established in full-time ministry, I became familiar with desperate times. Looking back, there were numerous opportunities to disobey God when He spoke to me about sowing seeds that were going to change my destiny. Here are the stories behind two remarkable harvests.

My miracle van: Years ago, I had saved up the money to trade my old vehicle in and purchase a new one debt-free. Back then, I drove to every one of my meetings. My old vehicle had several hundred thousand miles on it. I called it my miracle van—it was a miracle it made it from one meeting to the next!

The night before I was going to pick up a new van for our ministry, I was invited to sing on TBN. I was in Atlanta, Georgia with Jan Crouch. It was a telethon to raise money for the television ministry—it seems like just yesterday! Paul Crouch was uplinked with us, since he was in California.

He held up a piece of paper and said, "This is a license to build a TV station in Brazil that will preach the gospel seven days a week, twenty-four hours a day to millions of people. We can build this station for $250,000. That sounds like a lot of money, but it's only ten people giving $25,000 each."

That was the exact amount I had saved up to trade in my old miracle van and get my first vehicle debt-free. I did not come to the station that night to sow a $25,000 seed. I had never had that much money at one time, much less sowed that much money. But the moment Paul said, "ten people," I knew I was one of them. I tried to bargain with God. I tried to tell God I could not afford it.

I prayed that God would speak to someone else. I know His voice; I have heard it so many times. That $25,000 was no longer mine. When He spoke, that money became seed. I had two decisions. I could obey God, or I could disobey God.

My ministry was small back then—it was desperate times. Money and meetings were hard to come by, and I just went to smaller churches. It was a rare occasion that I got to sing on an international television program like TBN. I know now that *God did not have me there to sing, He had me there to sow*!

I wrote my check that night for $25,000, and I gave it to Jan. I told her not to read my name. I did not want people to think I had a lot of money. That was all the money I had.

It would take another book to tell you all the things God did after I sowed that seed. The first thing he did was to speak to Jan about filming some videos of my songs and playing them on TBN every day for over 12 years. She did not charge me a dime.

She also had Mike Purkey record several of the songs I had written or co-written on his music projects. My son Mark and I wrote "Let's Have Church" in about 10 minutes. That song opened a door for my music to be recorded and sung around the world. It launched my ministry into another dimension.

Paul and Jan Crouch were so kind and generous to me. I love and miss them both. Jan included me in things at TBN for several years. During that time, God opened doors to so many other television ministries—which are still open even to this day. Almost daily, I speak to the world on a television program somewhere.

A few weeks after I sowed the $25,000 seed, a man that I did not know called me. He said, "Brother Payne, God told me to contact you. I own a Chevrolet dealership in another state, and I was wondering if you could meet me there on Saturday at 2 p.m."

So, I drove my old miracle van to the dealership in the other state. When I got there, the man said, "I heard about what you did from someone at the TV station. There are three hundred and fifty fully customized vans out in that lot. Go pick out the one you want. The Lord told me to bless you with a van." I got the best one he had!

I ended up with a lot better van than I could have purchased with the seed God asked me for that night. Every two years for a number of years, I took the old van back and picked up a new one. After sowing that $25,000 for Christian television, I have never paid another car payment. Every vehicle since has been debt-free.

Precious seed for precious souls: I had a guitar that I loved to play. As I was playing it one day, the Lord spoke to me about the grandson of a pastor I knew. I was scheduled to go to that pastor's church for a three-day meeting. The Lord said to me, "When you go, take this guitar, and give it to the young man. There is a call on his life."

I hate to tell you this, but I took that guitar and put it in the closet. I piled clothes on it and stacked boxes up against it. Several weeks went by, and I did not play that guitar at all. I was hoping God would forget that He had spoken to me about this precious seed. I loved that guitar. About a week before I was to go to the church and preach, the Lord said to me, "Don't forget the guitar. Take it and have new strings put on it. Sow it into this young man's life.

I obeyed God, and I gave that young man my guitar. When I released that tough seed, revival broke out in that church and went on for several weeks. Many lives were touched. I also went back to that church at a later date, and this young man was on the platform playing that guitar. I was so glad I had obeyed the Lord. I can't tell you how good it felt to see that young man on the platform playing the guitar I had sown for Jesus!

There is something that happens supernaturally when you sow a seed in tough times. Are there seeds in your life that God has asked you to sow and you have not yet obeyed? The longer we delay our sowing, the longer we delay our harvest. Sowing in tough times proves that *when we do what is difficult, God does what is impossible.*

Against all odds and natural conditions, Isaac sowed. His seed did not know it was a time of famine. All his seed knew was that its destiny was to multiply. Your financial seed only knows what God has set in motion over it: God multiplies the seed that is sown!

Things To Remember From Chapter Eleven:

1. *When God gives you a direction, your answer not only affects you, but it will also affect your family for generations.*

2. *Seeds sown in times of devastation produce maximum multiplication.*

3. *You only attract what you expect. It takes a seed to activate the law of attraction.*

4. *God orchestrates your harvest, but your seed initiates your harvest.*

5. *Seeds are not moved by political problems, religious compromise, or even pandemics.*

6. *In the natural, the seed has to wait on the right season; in the kingdom, the right season is waiting on the seed. Your season is waiting on your seed!*

7. *Faith is determined by what you have left, not by what you released!*

CHAPTER 12

Seeing The Invisible

Words bring the unseen into the seen.

When a seed is planted in the ground, it becomes invisible to the natural eye. However, the picture on the package shows us what the harvest will look like. This is where faith is expressed. We must believe in something for which we only have a picture until it becomes a tangible, visible reality.

There is no greater example of faith. Words bring the invisible into the realm of the visible. God's Word is a seed. When it is spoken, it is sown. The results are not visible at the moment, but that spoken Word begins to create and bring the invisible into the realm of the visible and the intangible into the realm of the tangible.

> *Hebrews 11:1 (AMPC) Now faith is assurance, confirmation (the title deed) of things we hope for, being the proof of things we do not see.*

Faith perceives as fact that which has not yet been revealed to the five senses. You cannot see corn when it is growing beneath the earth, but it is creating a harvest that will, in time, become visible.

The one sure way to receive God's approval is to live your life by the unseen. The eleventh chapter of Hebrews has been called God's

Hall of Fame, and rightfully so. It is a collection of patriarchs in scripture who lived their lives by the invisible.

Here in Nashville where I live, we have the Country Music Hall of Fame. I have visited this place of history many times. On the wall, you can read the stories of how unknown singers rose from obscurity to become household names. You can see memorabilia such as cars, clothing, guitars, and other musical instruments. You can read of their accomplishments. It is a very enlightening place and an inspiration to people who play as well as listen to music.

I want to take you on a tour today through God's Hall of Fame. As we make our way through this journey you will see some remarkable similarities. Let's see some of these great men and women of God and read of their exploits:

Abel:
He brought God a more acceptable and better sacrifice than Cain.

Enoch:
He was caught up and did not face death.

Noah:
He built an ark though he had never seen rain.

Abraham:
He believed for a son for twenty-five years. That son was born when he was one hundred years old.

Sarah:
She was Abraham's wife. She received the power to bear a child long after she was past the time of conception.

Isaac:
He saw the future generations who would inherit the promises of God.

Jacob:
He blessed his children and prophesied their accomplishments as he died.

Esther:
She won a beauty pageant and became queen. She saved her nation from destruction.

Joseph:
He stayed true to God, even as he was sold into slavery by his brothers.

Moses:
He refused to be called the son of Pharaoh's daughter and became the deliverer of his people.

Rahab:
She hid God's servants and her life was spared.

Deborah:
She was a prophetess and judge of Israel who orchestrated victory over an oppressive king.

Saul:
He encountered Jesus on the Damascus road, was renamed Paul, and wrote a large portion of the New Testament.

Stephen:
He saw into the heavenlies as he faced martyrdom.

John:
He was persecuted and nearly died on the Isle of Patmos, but he lived to receive revelation from God.

So many other unknown and unnamed children of faith were able to undergo persecution and even death because they could see

Jesus (the invisible man) and trust Him with their soul. These are people who won God's approval by faith in the invisible.

Matthew, Mark, and Luke tell us the Word of God is a seed. A seed must be sown: that happens when the Word of God is spoken in faith. We know it is possible to move mountains by speaking the Word (Mark 11:23 KJV). When you speak the Word of God into a situation, you cannot see what is happening in the invisible realm, but the Word is working. Look at what this scripture says:

> *Hebrews 11:3 (AMPC) By faith we understand the worlds were formed and equipped for their intended purpose by the word of God. So that what you see was not made out of things that were visible.*

Everything we will ever need exists in the invisible. We can take the hand of faith, reach into the world of the invisible, and take hold of the intangible. Then, by faith, we hold on until the invisible becomes visible. Faith can bring the fourth dimension (invisible to the natural eye) into the third dimension (visible).

This is true when it comes to sowing financial seeds in the kingdom of God. We need to remember how things work when it comes to natural seeds. On the back of every seed packet such as corn, tomatoes, carrots, and beans, there are sowing instructions (how and when to plant).

In the kingdom, we have been given instructions on how and when to sow financial seeds and how to obtain a harvest. There are four important things when it comes to financial seeds and financial harvest:

1. Be led by the Holy Spirit in your sowing.

Do not give in to pressure, salesmanship, or sympathy. It is only the Holy Spirit who knows where and when we should sow. He will impress you. He will speak to you. He moves by peace, not pressure.

He moves by promise, not persuasion. He will point out what is on the other side of your sowing. He is not moved by need; He is only moved by the seed that is required to move us from fear to faith. We may plan to sow a certain seed, and He will let us know the correct amount. He will never lead you to sow in unproductive soil. If we listen to Him, we will always sow in good ground and reap one hundred-fold.

2. Never consider your resource, only your source.

Many people give what they can afford to give. While that is good economics, it is not good seedenomics. Faith does not operate in the realm of the comfortable, convenient, or conventional. Faith takes you beyond what you have grown accustomed to over the years. Faith is always leading you to a new level of *sowing* so that you can move to a new level of *reaping*. Our job is our *resource*; our God is our *source*. Our resources are *limited*; our source is *unlimited*.

3. Give with an expectancy to receive.

There is religious teaching that says we should never expect a harvest when we sow a seed! Let us refer again to the natural. What would a farmer say if I approached him while he was sowing wheat and said, "Mr. Farmer, you should never expect a harvest when you are sowing a seed." He would probably want to run me over with his tractor! The farmer not only expects a harvest, but he also expects to receive much more than he sows. The religious mindset says, "Well, that is different."

Is it? Let us look at what the Apostle Paul said to the church at Corinth when he was receiving an offering:

> *2 Corinthians 9:6 (KJV) He which sows sparingly, shall also reap sparingly.*

Notice Paul said, "If you sow a little, you will reap a little; if you sow a lot, you will reap a lot." Not one time did he suggest that you were not to expect a harvest when you sow. Still not convinced? Let's look further.

> *2 Corinthians 9:10 (NKJV) God gives seed to the sower.... then multiplies the seed sown!*

This verse explains that God multiplies the seed that we sow, and, in this context, He is talking about money. I have heard so many great Christians say, "I don't sow so I can reap, I just sow because I love God." That sounds humble and holy, but the truth is, it is completely opposed to the Word of God. God wants us to prosper, or He would have never given us the seed to sow. This is important because you only attract what you expect!

4. Pursue your harvest with all diligence.

In the natural, once seeds are sown, the battle begins to ensure a bountiful harvest. The farmer battles weeds, weather, birds, animals, and insects. When your seed is sown in the kingdom of God, you will battle impatience, fear, doubt, unbelief, and religion. If anything can talk you out of your harvest, it will.

Harvest is not automatic. Whether it is a natural harvest of tomatoes or a spiritual harvest of finances, it must be pursued. You must get up every morning and confess favor over your seed. You must bind the forces of hell that come to steal, kill, and destroy. You must keep your faith strong and your hope alive. Talk to your seed. Say, "I sowed you in faith and obedience to God's Word. I gave you an assignment. I command you in the name of Jesus to multiply and bring forth my harvest. I speak a hundredfold increase over you! You will not fail to bring forth." Then, praise God! Praise is like rain on a natural seed. It brings Holy Ghost rain on your kingdom seed.

Do not be moved by what things look like. Some people

miss their harvest because after they sow, the economy gets slow. Remember your seed and your Savior are not moved by the natural, they move in the supernatural. That is the major difference between economics and seedenomics. Praise God and watch what happens. Pursue with all diligence: you only possess what you are willing to pursue!

Real faith can see the invisible and accomplish the impossible:

> *Hebrews 11:6 (KJV) But without faith, it is impossible to please him: for he that cometh to God must believe that he is and that he is a rewarder of those who diligently seek him.*

Here we have the two dimensions of faith. One, *believe that God is.* Most people (and all devils) believe that God exists. The problem is that many people do not believe that God is a good God who wants to bless His people with abundance. This leads us to point two: *believe that God rewards those who seek Him.*

When it comes to seedenomics instead of economics, we must understand that seedenomics operates by faith. If faith is not present, then there will be no corresponding actions. Faith must be acted on to bring about the miraculous. You can say you have faith for abundance, riches, wealth, or to get out of debt, but your actions must express or demonstrate that type of faith. Look at what the book of James says:

> *James 2:14,17-19 (NIV) What good is it, my brothers and sisters, if someone claims to have faith but has no deeds? ... In the same way, faith by itself, if it is not accompanied by action, is dead. But someone will say, "You have faith; I have deeds." Show me your faith without deeds, and I will show you my faith by my deeds. You believe that there is one God. Good! Even the demons believe that—and shudder.*

Not too long ago, I was preaching at a large African American church. They were holding two services to accommodate the crowd. Between the first and second service, someone gave me ten one-hundred-dollar bills. I put them in my shirt pocket.

As I was preaching in the second service, I began to talk about the blessings of God and how God wanted to get His children out of debt and bring them into abundance. There was a great choir behind me, shouting "Amen!" and over a thousand people standing and clapping.

In the middle of all this, I said, "If you want this in your life, bring me a $1,000 seed! Everybody sat down. Nobody was excited anymore. The opportunity to step out in faith and change things suddenly moved them from emotions to reality. I just stopped preaching and stood there for about three minutes. The church fell silent.

Suddenly, a young lady from the choir walked up beside me and took out her checkbook. I stopped her and reached in my pocket and took out the ten one hundred dollars bills that had been invisible to the audience. I held them up for everyone to see. I said, "I didn't want the $1,000. I just wanted to identify the person God chose to receive this money."

Everyone had been given the same opportunity. The young lady who stepped out was unemployed and had been looking for a job. She had two children and a mortgage and was about to sow the last money she had in obedience to a man of God.

A young attorney who was visiting that day had just won a large lawsuit for one of his clients. When he saw this, he came forward after the service and asked me and the pastor if he could talk with us and the young lady.

We all went into the office, and he asked the young lady what she had made on her previous job. Then, he told her he would hire her and pay her twice as much as she had made before. He said, "You can work for me until you find something better." It worked out so well that she stayed on with him. He later paid her house off because of her good work. All this happened because she was willing to sow a seed in faith.

Our words and actions direct the course of our lives toward success or failure. Words are seeds that always produce a harvest! Words bring the invisible into the visible realm.

Things To Remember From Chapter Twelve:

1. One sure way to receive God's approval is to live your life by the unseen.

2. We reach into the world of the invisible and take hold of the intangible. Then, by faith, we hold on until the invisible becomes visible.

3. Faith does not operate in the realm of the comfortable, convenient, or conventional.

4. Our job is our *resource*; our God is our *source*.

5. Your seed and your Savior are not moved by the natural, they move in the supernatural.

6. Seedenomics operates by faith.

7. Words bring the invisible into the visible realm.

CHAPTER 13

Poor Vs. Rich

. . . .

Poverty Mentality vs. Seedenomics Mentality

. . . .

To have a seedenomics mentality, a poverty mentality must be broken. Poverty is a prison. Poverty holds more people in bondage than all other prisons combined. There are no gray stone walls or steel bars, but it is a prison, nonetheless.

This prison holds single mothers who are trying to make enough money to feed and clothe their children. This prison holds fathers who don't see any way out of the poverty cycle that binds them. This prison holds businessmen who don't believe they are worthy of success. This prison holds churchgoers who hold back their tithe because they can't seem to make ends meet.

There are also many other inmates from every walk of life locked in this prison. Each one is living with a life sentence of poverty because they bought the lie that said, "You are always going to be poor."

The way a person becomes poor is by their mentality, the way they think. An acronym for the word *poor* is Passing Over Opportunities Repeatedly:

P   (*passing*)

O   (*over*)

O   (*opportunities*)

R   (*repeatedly*)

When you hear and learn the principles, yet pass by the opportunities you have to sow, you become poor. Once you are poor, you handcuff your future and you are locked into poverty. Information without application leads to the mind's incarceration.

Poverty is Satan's curse on humanity because of sin, but he must come through doorways that have been opened by individuals. He comes through these open doors and imposes his will over humanity's will.

Prosperity is God's will and desire for our lives. But these doorways are roadblocks to God's will of prosperity for you. God's Word is God's will. Look at what God said about His will concerning material blessings:

> *3 John 2 (KJV) Beloved, I wish above all things, that you may prosper and be in health, even as your soul prospers.*

God put prosperity before health when He states His will for His children.

> *Psalm 35:27 (NKJV) Let the Lord be magnified, Who has pleasure in the prosperity of his servant.*

. . . .

Doorways That Allow Poverty In Your Life

. . . .

After forty-six years, I have discovered three things that allow a poverty spirit to have access to the mind. Satan must be given access; he does not have the power to take it.

1. An Unteachable Spirit

> *Proverbs 13:18 (NKJV) says, Poverty and shame shall be to him that refuses instruction.*

An unteachable person hears but neither receives nor acts on the information they have been given. It is not that they cannot learn—they just refuse to be taught.

I talk to people weekly and share with them the steps that I used to get out of debt. I also offer the teaching on CD. The people I talk to gladly listen and even agree with what I tell them. But for some, there is no change. They take no action to free themselves from the prison of debt.

A teachable person is willing to change once they have been shown a better way. An unteachable person resists change because change is painful. A teachable person knows that *you must give up the way things are, to have things the way you want them to be.*

We were so poor when I was a child that we did not go on vacation. Dad would sit us in the car and hold up pictures of what we would have seen, had we been able to put the money together to go. My mom and dad were good hard-working people, but no one had ever taught them how to break the cycle of poverty that had been passed down to them by their parents.

Having been raised in poverty, I was eager for someone to teach me how I could break this cycle in my life. Once I was exposed to the necessary information, I quickly embraced it and allowed it to open my prison of poverty and set me free.

> *Proverbs 24:4 (AMPC) By knowledge shall your chambers be filled with all precious and pleasant riches.*

Knowledge is power over the cycle of poverty. Third John 2 tells us our souls (mind, will, and emotions) must prosper before our hands prosper. Knowledge determines how you think, reason, and respond to teaching about prosperity. Knowledge is essential if you want to achieve prosperity.

Proverbs 23:7 (KJV) As a man thinks in his heart so is he.

The power of God for prosperity seldom rises above man's level of thinking. Poverty mentality manifests in the following manner:

- *It resists thoughts of wealth and abundance.*
- *It turns a deaf ear to Biblical teachings concerning the accumulation and management of money.*
- *It makes excuses for lack, need, and want.*
- *It rejects any idea that things can change, and they can be free from financial insufficiency.*
- *It becomes angry at teaching that promises blessings for obedient giving.*

To prosper, you must first break the cycle of poverty thinking. Use these three steps to renew your mind.

1. *RECOGNIZE poverty thoughts.*
2. *DESTROY poverty thoughts.*
3. *REPLACE poverty thoughts with thoughts of prosperity.*

These steps seem simple. But they will lead you out of a poverty mindset into a prosperity mindset.

2. Laziness

Proverbs 24:33,34 (KJV) Yet a little sleep, a little slumber, a little folding of the hands to sleep: So shall poverty come as one that travails and wants as an armed man.

To succeed and prosper, you must be willing to work, and work hard. The majority of people I talk to hate their job. Consequently, they do not put their heart into their work, and many drift from job to job. They develop a negative attitude toward their job and employer. They drink coffee, take breaks, and kill time. All these are characteristics of laziness.

One thing has always amazed me about this great land of opportunity that we know as America. Many of the people who are born here work for people who came here from other countries. Almost all hotels that I stay in are owned by entrepreneurs from other countries. It appears that people who have never had a chance at success are willing to work harder than people who were born in the middle of opportunity. Ninety percent of the time, the difference between being average, mediocre, or successful is your work ethic.

People who have an old car and refuse to keep it clean seldom get a new car. People who live in an old house where the weeds need cut down, the trim needs painted, the broken windows need replaced, and the gutters need cleaned, seldom get a better house. The reason is laziness.

There's an old saying, "The early bird gets the worm." That is what the writer of the proverbs is saying. A little sleep, a little slumber, and poverty and want come like an armed man.

Everyone on earth has the same amount of time in a day. Twenty-four hours: fourteen hundred and forty minutes. You can spend time, waste time, or invest time. But the thing about time you must not forget is it does not wait, and it cannot be reclaimed.

Now is the time to begin to move your finances to a new level. Do not quit the job you hate. Work harder there than you have ever worked. In the meantime, educate yourself for a better job. Find a way to start your own business. Set goals and begin to work toward those goals.

Unfinished projects, unread books, and unfulfilled dreams are the characteristics of laziness. And only you can change that pattern and break that cycle. It's never too late to be great.

3. Disobedience

Many people live in poverty because of acts of disobedience when it comes to money. The Bible is very clear when it comes to the handling of money. It teaches that the first 10% of one's income should be given to the Lord's work as a tithe.

> *Malachi 3:10-11 (KJV) Bring ye all the tithes into the storehouse, that there may be meat in mine house, and prove me now herewith, saith the LORD of hosts, if I will not open you the windows of heaven, and pour you out a blessing, that there shall not be room enough to receive it. And I will rebuke the devourer for your sakes, and he shall not destroy the fruits of your ground; neither shall your vine cast her fruit before the time in the field, saith the LORD of hosts.*

The tithe puts God above us. The tithe says we have conquered our greed, and we trust God with our money. Many people look at the tithe as a law they must keep, and they resist it. Others look at the tithe as something that was practiced in the Old Testament and does not apply to us today.

Most people who have this attitude never experience real prosperity. I am not going to condemn anyone for their financial practices. That is between you and God. But I do want to share with you my personal experience.

When I was first saved, I made $52.00 a week. Now I have been saved a long time. When I was told I needed to tithe, I rejected it for a few weeks. Finally, a good friend of mine showed me from the

Bible that it was the right thing to do. I remember that my first tithe was $5.20. Gas was twenty-five cents a gallon back then. That meant my tithe was more than a tankful of gas.

God began to bless me financially in a matter of weeks. I have continued that practice all these years, and I have never wanted for any good thing in life. I know God's Word is true, and you can take it to the bank.

I learned if I am going to be rich, I must begin to practice the principles I learned from reading God's Word. God gave me an acronym for the word *rich*—Receiving Instruction Concerning Harvest:

R (*receiving*)

I (*instruction*)

C (*concerning*)

H (*harvest*)

God's will is for all of us to be rich and prosperous.

Ephesians 3:20 (KJV) Now unto him that is able!

Philippians 4:19 (KJV) My God shall supply all your needs!

Prosperity is God's plan. Seedenomics is God's will for us to apply in our lives. To apply seedenomics, we must develop a seedenomics mindset. What is a seedenomics mindset?

A Seedenomics Mindset

To develop a seedenomics mindset, read these statements aloud daily. Memorize them and recite them aloud to expand your mind and build your faith. The more you rehearse these seven statements, the more you will develop a seedenomics mentality.

1. *God's plan for my life is abundance.*
2. *God's laws and principles are designed to produce abundance.*
3. *Abundance allows for choices.*
4. *I control my level of increase by the seeds I sow and the soil I sow into.*
5. *I am a sower—I live to sow. I am always looking for places to sow.*
6. *There will never be a day in my life when I have no seeds to sow.*
7. *I expect a harvest when I release a seed. If it is corn, I expect corn. If it is money, I expect money.*

Things To Remember From Chapter Thirteen:

1. *Poor is P-passing O-over O-opportunities R-repeatedly.*

2. *Poverty is Satan's curse on humanity because of sin.*

3. *Prosperity is God's will and desire for our lives.*

4. *You must give up the way things are, to have things the way you want them to be.*

5. *Knowledge is power over the cycle of poverty. Knowledge is essential to achieve prosperity.*

6. *Rich is R-receiving I-instructions C-concerning H-harvest.*

7. *Seedenomics is the ability to connect to the supernatural provision of God through a seed.*

PART V

CONCLUSION AND APPLICATION

. . . . . .

CHAPTER 14

The Sustainer's Seed

1 Kings 17: 9 (KJV) I have commanded
a widow woman there to sustain thee.

. . . .

Two Sticks, A Handful Of Meal, and a Little Oil

. . . .

This story could very well be a Broadway play or a Hollywood mini-series. Suggested titles would include "The Widow," "The Miracle at Zarephath" or "The Bottom of The Barrel." It is a story of tragedy turned into triumph.

As the curtain rises and the orchestra begins to play, we find the widow in her kitchen staring at a meal barrel and a cruse of oil that are almost empty. A woman with daring faith is down to her last meal. She faces the possibility of death, not only hers but also her son's.

The widow's humble dwelling sits on the outskirts of Zarephath. An extended famine has filled the air with the stench of death. She's attended many funerals of family and friends. Hunger pains and fear fill the eyes of those who are left. I can see this poor widow standing on a cold stone floor. She is very thin and frail—nothing more than skin draped over bone.

The lines in her face are signatures of days of intense struggle. Her eyes are hollow and set deep in her head, contrasted only by the dark circles. For days now, the grim reaper has been knocking on her door. He has an invitation for her and her son to join him at a party in their honor, a party called death. She has fought him off for as long as she can. One more meal and it will all be over.

She is at the end, and as anyone at the end would do, she begins to pray. The widow reaches into the crude clay meal barrel and gathers every grain of meal in her hand and lifts it up to God. Then with the other hand, she picks up the cruse of cooking oil. Her prayer went something like this; "Oh, God of Abraham, Isaac, and Jacob, I have served you all these many years. You have never failed me. I can't wait any longer, send prosperity now!

Desperation is at her door. With every passing second, hope is being extinguished. She is standing between death and deliverance. She is at the bottom of her barrel.

Then, God spoke to her. He told her that He would be sending her a prophet, and that she should sustain him. While speaking to her, God also spoke to the prophet and told him that He has commanded a widow to sustain him. To *sustain* means to care for, support, or prolong life for an extended period. *At this moment, her response to God's command will determine God's response to her demand.*

She can obey the voice of God, or she can eat her last meal, and she and her son will die. What will make the difference in the widow's life? The same thing that will make the difference in our lives: obedience to the word God speaks to us.

If you are going to see miraculous provision now, like the widow, you must observe these seven principles:

. . . .

One: Hear And Obey The Word That God Gives You

. . . .

You must follow the Word of God spoken to you. Take the other character in the story, Elijah. Elijah is a prophet with a crusty exterior. His hair is long and unkempt. His skin is weathered from the desert heat and night winds. His beard is turning gray and could use a trim. He wears a leather mantel around his shoulders and his voice sounds like thunder on a spring day.

It was this prophet's anger against an unrighteous king that caused this famine. There is no record that God told Elijah to shut up heaven. Elijah was acting on his own! We see here that God always honors the words of His prophets. I am talking about true prophets, not the self-proclaimed prophets of today. They prophesy political outcomes of elections and when they miss it, they try to explain away their error! They give true prophets a bad name.

King Ahab and his wife Jezebel had torn down God's altars, paid off his prophets, and formed unholy alliances to destroy God's people. Elijah prayed and God shut up heaven, and the sky refused to give forth rain for three and a half years. But God had a plan to sustain Elijah. The Bible says that God began to speak to him:

> *1 Kings 17:2–3 (KJV) And the word of the Lord came unto him, saying, Get thee hence, and turn thee eastward, and hide thyself by the brook Cherith, that is before Jordan.*

God told Elijah to go to a certain brook. In obedience, Elijah went and camped down by the brook called Cherith, which means a place of breaking off in Hebrew. There were some things that would be broken off Elijah in that place.

When God is ready to move anyone from the natural to the supernatural, He breaks off things that would keep them from His blessings. God wanted to get Elijah to that place of dependence that could only happen at Cherith. God wanted Elijah to know that when God is your total source, you have God's total supply.

Elijah was in a famine, and God sent him to a place where only He could meet the need. God will often direct us like He did Elijah—to a place where we must exhaust *everything* in the natural to experience *anything* in the supernatural! Elijah had to get where God was sending him.

We, also, must be obedient like Elijah. Following the word God speaks to us will put us in a position to receive His provision.

. . . .

Two: There Is A Place Where God Commands His Blessing

. . . .

2 Kings 17:4 (KJV) And it shall be, that thou shalt drink of the brook; and I have commanded the ravens to feed thee there.

There was a specific place where God commanded the ravens to feed Elijah; there is a specific place where God commands His blessings to come to us. If God can whisper in a raven's ear to prosper a prophet, He can whisper to an employer to promote you and give you a raise. He can direct you to the place where He has assigned your blessing. Listen and obey His commands. There is a place called "There" for your life.

When I read this story, I marvel at the power of God. At that time, the only place to find meat during this famine was on the king's table. To provide for Elijah, God sent the ravens to the palace, had them pick up dinner, and take it to the prophet. Instead of "Domin-os," God had "Raven-os." God was able to deliver sustenance through unusual sources.

God moves quickly when we get to the place where He has commanded His blessing. When Elijah arrived at the right place, the blessing was there. Has God spoken to you about your place called "There"? If so, move now! Many are not blessed because they are in a place of disobedience, not in their place called "There."

Two people may sit in the same church. Both hear the same messages. God speaks to each individual about sowing a seed. One responds and does what God tells them to do. The other leaves and remains in disobedience. Isn't it obvious why one is blessed and the other lives under the curse of want, lack, and need?

> *Deuteronomy 28:1 (KJV) And it shall come to pass, if thou shalt hearken diligently unto the voice of the Lord thy God, to observe and to do all his commandments which I command thee this day, that the Lord thy God will set thee on high above all nations of the earth:*

If you will obey, God will command His blessings. The commanded blessings depend on your obedience. I want you to know:

- *You were born to be blessed!*
- *You can be blessed!*
- *God wants to bless you right now!*

To walk these blessings out, you must get yourself to the place called "There" for your life. You ask, "Where is my "There"? It is the place He has prepared provision for you. If you don't know where your "There" is, pray and ask God to direct you. Get yourself to that place through obedience and watch what God will do.

. . . .

Three: Don't Sit Beside A Dry Brook!

. . . .

> *1Kings 17:7 (KJV) And it came to pass after a while, the brook dried up...*

The place of God's blessing today may not be the place of God's blessing tomorrow. One day the brook is flowing, and the ravens are flying. The next day the brook is dry, and the ravens are on strike.

Elijah could pray, "Lord, let this brook flow again. Lord, let your blessings rest here again." Or, he could discern that God had dried up the brook.

Put yourself in Elijah's shoes. It must have been tough to look at the dry brook and wonder where the water went. Have you ever been beside a dry brook asking why? Don't feel bad, everyone has ridden the roller coaster of blessings and burdens. Crisis and pain come to us all at some point in our lives. The sun does not shine every day. The lesson we must learn is that pain can be a great motivator. When the pain of remaining the same becomes greater than the pain of change, we will change.

There are times when God will let the brook dry up. I hear you asking me, "Bishop Payne, why do brooks dry up?" I believe it is to let us know that God is still the one who controls the rain. Elijah is learning this lesson. Elijah had been sitting at the brook taking it easy, but now this place of miracles is a place of memories. All that remains is the remembrance of better times. Elijah finds himself in a place of shortage. The shortage is a signal that something must change. Standing in the sand of a dry brook, the Word of the Lord came to Elijah again:

1 Kings 17:8–9 (KJV) And the word of the Lord came unto him saying, Arise…

Elijah had a choice to make. He could stay where he was and reminisce about what used to be, or *he could chart a new course to a new source.* The same is true for us. We can stay beside a dry brook praying for God to change His mind, or we can go where He is leading. I have talked with so many believers who have arrived at the end of their faith and found themselves beside a dry brook.

God speaks to them to go to a certain church. They go in obedience, and when they arrive, they are blessed. God pours out His Spirit, the blessings are flowing, and things are going great. Then, after a few years, the church dries up and dies, but they remain because of relationships. They stay there and end up dying spiritually because they remained by a dry brook.

Now don't misunderstand me, there are times when we all face dry seasons because of our failure to hear the Word of the Lord. It is in these times we need to pray for wisdom to hear God's voice and move on with God. One single act of obedience now can bring you into a season of blessings. Here is the word I want to impart to you: *don't stay where the water (spirit) is not flowing.*

It is a tragedy that millions have died sitting beside a dry brook. I want to shout it from the mountain tops: NO MORE DRY BROOKS! NO MORE DRY BROOKS! I wrote this chapter for anyone whose finances have dried up; it is time to hear the word of the Lord.

I have people writing to me all the time, wishing they could hear from God. I want you to know you are hearing from God right now. He is speaking to you through the words on this page. Here's your word: *if you stay where you are, you are going to die beside your dry brook.*

Get up right now; get going! God is waiting on you. Cry out, "No more dry brooks!" Every miracle begins with the first step of faith. It was a six-mile walk from Cherith to Zarephath, but that was the place of Elijah's next miracle. One step away from defeat is one step toward victory. One step away from debt, lack, and financial adversity is one step toward a debt-free life of abundance and blessing.

. . . .

Four: Listen And Follow The Voice Of God Speaking Through A Man Of God.

. . . .

As the widow watched each grain of meal sift between her fingers and fall back into her small meal barrel, she heard a voice. The voice said, "You are not going to make it. You are going to die."

She recognized that voice—it was the voice of need. That voice produces:

- *Fear*
- *Worry*
- *Panic*
- *Doubt*

- *Doubt*
- *Anxiety*
- *Unbelief*
- *Death*

In your mind, can you see this poor widow? Right in the middle of her darkest hour, at the point of decision, need is telling her, "This is it, it's about to be over."

When all of the sudden out of the darkness, she hears another voice. This voice is the one that resounded in Genesis, "Let there be light!" and there was light. This voice spoke creation into being—this was the voice of God Almighty. God whispered to a widow who was down to her last meal. He said, "There is a man of God coming to your house today, do what he tells you to do. Sustain him with your seed!"

The time of decision has come for her. She is standing at the gate with two sticks in her hand, the long wait is over. Today is the day of her deliverance. Her answer is coming from the same lips that caused the problem. His exterior is rough, and he looks like a vagabond. The widow, however, is more interested in the content than the package. It is his words that her heart hungers to hear. She knows he is the mouthpiece of God. Don't miss this great truth: *the key to your harvest is in the mouth of a servant of God.*

We need to learn a valuable lesson from this widow before we proceed to her miracle. Servants of God today may come packaged differently than Elijah. They may wear designer clothes, carry an expensive briefcase, have an entourage, and fly in their own jet. But if they have a proven ministry, and they are a minister of character, then they may be the only thing that stands between you and destruction—so listen and obey their words. Notice what Elijah spoke to the widow:

1 Kings 17:10–11 (KJV) Fetch me, I pray thee, a little water in a vessel, that I might drink. And as she was going to fetch it, he called to her, and said, Bring me, I pray thee, a morsel of bread in thine hand.

The words from this man of God were not what she wanted to hear. Instead of building faith, they were feeding fear. Immediately, she began to make excuses. "I do not have a cake. What I have belongs to me and my son. We are going to eat it and die."

Even after God told her to sustain this prophet with her seed, she had problems obeying. Before we condemn her, let us ask ourselves, "How many times have we done the same thing when God spoke to us about a seed?"

We have said, "No, we can't afford to. No, that's not me He's talking to. No, now is not a good time." Our refusals break God's heart because they put His blessings on hold. He cannot bless disobedience. When we say *no* to God, He is forced to say *no* to us.

I know this hurts God when He can't give us what He desires to give us. As a parent of two boys and three awesome grandchildren, my greatest desire is to give them good things. There have been times in the past however when I have had to withhold blessings. These were painful times for me because I missed the joy of giving. I know our Heavenly Father feels the same way. He wants to bless us, but we tie His hands when we are not obedient to His commands.

. . . .

Five: Put God And His Ministries First

. . . .

1 Kings 17:13 (KJV) Bake me a little cake first…

Elijah would have been the hottest topic of his day, had he lived in the era of social media. Can you imagine the posts about this man of God? I can hear them now. *A homeless, self-proclaimed prophet takes a poor widow's last meal, leaving her and her son to die of hunger.*

You could have read the one-sided account on the front cover of every magazine in the checkout line of your local grocery. This type of reporting today is a strategy of Satan. It is designed to intimidate servants of God. It's purpose is to cast suspicion on the believer and make the words of a prophet suspect.

When this happens, prosperity and blessing are hindered in the church. This type of reporting was birthed in the pit of hell. Listen to the spirit of God in you. He will bear witness with your spirit when God is speaking through man. God spoke to the widow one on one, and then through the prophet.

God has a different point of view. He sends a servant of God with an assignment to *take what is necessary to produce what is needed.* Elijah was sent to challenge the widow to use her faith. It was necessary for Elijah to bring her to the place of decision. The widow had to make a choice. She can put herself first and have a meal, or she can put God first and have a miracle.

God uses the same plan today. It may be a pastor, an evangelist, or a television minister. But someone is going to come to you with a word from God . . .

- *to challenge you to give God your best gift*
- *to sow a seed you have never sown*
- *to reap a harvest you have never known*

You are faced with the same dilemma as the widow. Do I plant my seed in the face of my need? We must make this same decision every time God speaks to us to plant a seed.

As a man of God, I weep each month as I read the letters from my partners. Several live on fixed incomes. One precious saint in Texas sends me one hundred dollars a month. Her letters touch my heart—another widow who puts God first. God is her source, and

He meets her needs. She has told me that she knows she would be dead if it were not for her giving.

I know these precious partners have a special place in the heart of God. Millions like these saints keep the work of God moving forward. They are modern-day believers with faith like the widow of Zarephath. To these, the church and every great ministry owe eternal gratitude. This is the reason I pray and spend God's money wisely to touch as many lives as possible with the Word of God.

. . . .

Six: Use Your Faith, Refuse Your Fear

. . . .

Hebrews 11:6 (NKJV) But without faith, it is impossible to please Him. For he who comes to God must believe that He is and that He is a rewarder of those who diligently seek him.

The widow's palms were sweaty, her heart was beating fast, and her mind was rebelling like a teenager sitting down to a pile of homework. Why? She's using her faith and refusing her fear. Is she afraid? Of course! Fear does not sit down when faith stands up. Every great miracle happens with fear and faith pulling the heartstrings of a believer like a rope in a tug of war. Fear immobilizes the believer; fear paralyzes the hand of God. He is a God who is moved only by faith.

One of the greatest revelations I ever received came one day as I was praying over my need. As I was telling God about how serious my situation was, He spoke these words to me: "My *heart is moved* by your need, but my *hand is moved* by your seed." It was then I realized that the widow had to bake the cake. God could do nothing until she did something. The hunger and the empty meal barrel moved his heart. That was the reason He sent Elijah. But His hand was moved when she made her last cake a seed.

You will have to use your faith and refuse your fear. Decide right now to do something for God's work that will require you to use your faith. If you desire to live free from debt and financial adversity, you must move beyond the comfort zone. You must stop giving what is convenient or comfortable. If your seed doesn't move you, it will not move God.

. . . .

Seven: Your Obedience Today Will Determine Your Options Tomorrow

. . . .

Have you ever wondered what would have happened if Elijah had refused to obey God? Would God have sent someone else to challenge the widow to use her faith? Probably not. She and her son would have eaten their last meal and died. Can you see the importance of the ministers who are sent to you by the Lord? They come with a message to challenge you to use your faith.

God honors the prophetic words they speak. When a man of God receives your seed and prophesies prosperity now, prosperity will come quickly. This poor widow went from the bottom of the barrel to a year's supply of meal and oil all because of her obedience to the word of a man of God.

What if the widow had refused to bake the cake and feed the man of God? Would he have died? When I ask this question, most people believe God would have sent someone else. I don't believe that. I believe Elijah would have died. Israel would not have repented and turned back to God under his ministry. The ones who disagree with me usually use their belief to excuse themselves from obeying God when He tells them to give their best. If we believe someone else will take care of God's ministers and ministry, we will not obey.

Some of you who are reading these words are almost out of options. If you continue to refuse to obey God, you will live under the curse of disobedience. Bow your head right now. Ask God what

He would have you sow right now concerning this ministry God has entrusted to me. I am your Elijah today. God has sent me to you through the words you are reading. Now I want to challenge you to use the envelope in the back of this book. God is calling you to be a sustainer, to sow a sustainer's seed! Send your best seed today for souls. Do not sow according to your resources. God is your source. Do exactly what He tells you to do. When I hold your seed in my hand, I will prophesy as David did:

Psalms 118:25 (KJV) Save now, I beseech thee, Lord: O Lord, I beseech thee, send now prosperity.

Things to remember from Chapter Fourteen:

1. Hear and obey the word that God gives to you.

2. "There" is a place where God commands His blessings.

3. Don't sit by a dry brook. Chart a new course to a new source.

4. Obey the voice of God through a man of God for your life. Keep God's ministries first.

5. When we say no to God, He is forced to say no to us.

6. Use your faith; refuse your fear.

7. Your obedience today will determine your options tomorrow.

Application

The information you have read in this book is just information unless it is applied. You can take the principles in this book and apply them, or you can pass over them. You can pass over opportunities and remain poor, or you can receive instructions concerning harvest and become rich. I choose to be rich. I am going to listen to the Holy Spirit's instruction and sow when He tells me to sow. I know that when I sow, seedenomics goes into action in my life.

Seedenomics is the ability to connect to the supernatural provision of God through a seed. When you get the power of seedenomics operating in your life, you will go from lack to abundance. You will go from being a casual giver into being a true sower. You will start looking for opportunities to sow, and you will be able to recognize opportunities for seed to be sown. The principles that you have learned in this book will change your life. I know that because seedenomics has changed my life.

I want to thank you for reading this book and I pray that what you have read has given you hope and instruction on how to live a seedenomics life. I believe that God is going to use this as a tool to raise up the next generation of sowers. I am excited about hearing from the new sowers who are being birthed because of this revelation.

I look forward to connecting with you. Please use the envelope in this book to stay connected with me. Sow a seed to help us take this message of seedenomics to the world. I can't wait to hear the testimonies about what seedenomics is doing for you and your family. May the Lord bless you richly in favor and prosperity.

Seedenomics Decision Page

My greatest desire is for you to prosper and be in health. You can go to heaven broke, and you can go sick—but you cannot go lost!

So, I must ask you this question: If you were to die today, are you ready to meet Jesus? Have you asked Jesus to come into your heart and be your personal Savior? Please understand this is not joining a church or turning over a new leaf or trying to do better. I was bound by sin. I was an alcoholic and a drug addict and had never been to church. When I gave my soul to Jesus, He gave me a life worth living. He delivered me from all the addictions.

No one can make this decision for you. You must ask Jesus to come into your heart yourself. Here is what the Bible says about Jesus:

John 3:16 (KJV) *For God so loved the world (that is us) that He gave His only begotten son (Jesus) that whoever would believe on Him should not perish but have everlasting life (emphasis added).*

Romans 10:9 (NKJV) *If you confess with your mouth the Lord Jesus and believe in your heart that God raised Him from the dead, you would be saved.*

Romans 10:13 *(NKJV) For whoever calls on the name of the Lord shall be saved.*

> ***To receive Jesus as your Lord and Savior,***
> ***please pray the following prayer with me:***

Salvation Prayer

Dear Jesus,

I believe you are the son of God. I believe you died on a cross, were buried in a tomb, and rose from the dead. I am a sinner, and I cannot save myself. I come to you today and ask you for forgiveness of all my sins.

I confess you with my mouth today, and I believe in my heart that I am saved. I will follow you in water baptism, I will receive your gift of the Holy Spirit, and I will testify to others about my salvation. Thank you, Jesus, for saving me!

Yes, James, I prayed this prayer today and I have accepted Jesus as my personal Lord and Savior. I will find a church and keep my commitment to follow Jesus. I will live in the peace of God and make Heaven my eternal home!

Name: _____

Email: _____

Facebook: _____

Twitter: _____

Please write to me and let me know how you are doing. I would also like to stay connected with you.

Follow me on Facebook and Twitter @drjamespayne.

Seedenomics Partnership Page

Dear Partner,

God through this book has brought us together for such a time as this. Alone we can do little, but together we can do much for God's kingdom. Will you be a faith partner with me? Your seed can touch lives around the world. You always partake of what you partner with!

This is a debt-free ministry. This is fertile ground for sowing seed and receiving a hundred-fold harvest! You can expect a Luke 6:38 blessing. Pressed down, shaken together, and running over, men will give to you.

Social Media: @DrJamesPayne
CashApp: $drjamespayne
JamesPayneMinistries.com

I promise to pray over your seed each day and prophesy your harvest!

*Please connect with me today by completing the form and mail it with your seed today! You can also text your gift to **(731) 506-0734**. Follow me on Facebook and Twitter @drjamespayne.*

Your Faith Partner
Dr. James Payne

Sowing Opportunities

☐ **365 Seedenomics Partner.** James, I will give a one-time gift of $365.00 or $30.00 per month. I believe a seed-a-day will result in a harvest each day!

☐ **638 Seedenomics Partner.** James, I will give a one-time gift of $638, or I will send $54.00 per month. I am enclosing my first $54.00. *This gift will activate Luke 6:38! We have seen numerous miracles when people sow this amount!*

☐ **1000 Seedenomics Partner.** James, I will give a one-time gift of $1,000 to break the back of debt, lack, and need in my life, or I will send $84 per month. *I believe what God did for me, He will do for you. We have seen Him do this over and over!*

☐ **One-Time Gift.** James, I will give as the Holy Spirit directs me. Please accept my gift of _____ today!

TOTAL ENCLOSED | $ _____

NAME: _____

ADDRESS: _____

CITY: _____

STATE: _____ ZIP: _____

PHONE: _____

EMAIL: _____

MAILING ADDRESS:

JAMES PAYNE MINISTRIES INC.
P.O. BOX 39
EAGLEVILLE, TN 37060

You can get your seed in faster by texting to (731)506-0734.

It is secure and safe. All donations are tax-deductible. Accounting by Chitwood and Chitwood, Chattanooga, Tennessee.

2 Corinthians 9:10 (NKJV) Now may He who supplies seed to the sower, and bread for food, supply and multiply the seed you have sown and increase the fruits of your righteousness.

Printed in the United States
by Baker & Taylor Publisher Services